I Believe in The Holy Spirit?

I Believe in The Holy Spirit?

Arthur X. Deegan II, PhD

I BELIEVE IN THE HOLY SPIRIT?
Copyright © 2019 by Arthur X. Deegan II, PhD

Library of Congress Control Number: 2019900263
ISBN-13:   Paperback: 978-1-950073-39-9
           PDF: 978-1-950073-40-5
           ePub: 978-1-950073-41-2
           Kindle: 978-1-950073-42-9

All rights reserved. No part of this publication may be reproduced, distributed, or transmitted in any form or by any means, including photocopying, recording, or other electronic or mechanical methods, without the prior written permission of the publisher or author, except in the case of brief quotations embodied in critical reviews and certain other noncommercial uses permitted by copyright law.

Although every precaution has been taken to verify the accuracy of the information contained herein, the author and publisher assume no responsibility for any errors or omissions. No liability is assumed for damages that may result from the use of information contained within.

Printed in the United States of America

GoToPublish LLC
1-888-337-1724
www.gotopublish.com
info@gotopublish.com

Contents

Dedication	vii
ACKNOWLEDGMENTS	ix
ACKNOWLEDGMENT	xi
FOREWORD	xiii
WHAT DOES THE HOLY SPIRIT DO?	**1**
Spirit versus Holy Spirit	9
Holy Spirit versus Holy Ghost	11
Author's Note	14
THE HOLY SPIRIT AS BREATH OF LIFE	**15**
He creates life	15
He gives right order	20
He causes rebirth	22
He baptizes	25
He can end life	26
Conclusion	29
A BRIEF CONVERSATION WITH THE HOLY SPIRIT	29
THE HOLY SPIRIT AS INSPIRER	**33**
He inspires our thoughts and words	34
He gives a new mind	35
He helps us understand scripture (which he wrote)	37
He inspires prophets	44
He inspires in the New Testament	48
He gives gifts and fruits	53
He teaches us how to pray	56
Conclusion	58
A BRIEF CONVERSATION WITH THE HOLY SPIRIT	58

THE HOLY SPIRIT AS LOVER — 61
- He unites through love — 61
- He consoles, comforts — 67
- He attracts us only to what is holy — 71
- He speaks through images — 75
- Conclusion — 79
- A BRIEF CONVERSATION WITH THE HOLY SPIRIT — 80

THE HOLY SPIRIT AS HELPER — 83
- He empowers — 83
- He consecrates Priests, Prophets and Kings — 86
- He gives Charisms — 91
- He gives Baptism of the Spirit — 92
- He helps discernment of one's life work — 96
- Conclusion — 99
- A BRIEF CONVERSATION WITH THE HOLY SPIRIT — 99

THE HOLY SPIRIT AS PROTECTOR — 103
- He takes up his dwelling within us — 103
- He protects from illness and suffering — 105
- He guides along the way — 107
- He provides strength — 111
- He rescues us — 113
- He protects the true faith — 113
- Conclusion — 119
- A BRIEF CONVERSATION WITH THE HOLY SPIRIT — 119

A Final Word ... — 123

Dedication

In loving memory of my

Parents and Grandparents,

whose faithful passing down

of the true faith,

has inspired this study

of the Holy Spirit

ACKNOWLEDGMENTS

I am writing principally to my Catholic brothers and sisters. For that reason I do not hesitate to cite the bible first, then our Catholic catechism, various encyclicals of the popes and the documents from Vatican Council 11 as "arguments" from authority. At the same time, I trust adherents to other religious communities will also find these sources worthy of some weight in considering my conclusions.

I write not as a student of the Hebrew, Aramaic or other language of the bible. I leave the discussions (and controversies) about the various possible meanings of the text to the experts. I choose to follow the translation in the latest version of the New American Bible, drawn mainly from the Vulgate of St. Jerome, though I maintain the right to quote some of those experts to explain one passage or other as needed.

Any Concordance of the bible will provide the reader with the thousands of times the Spirit is referred to in the many books of both the Old and New Testaments. The Pentecostal movement has provided several authors who have compiled groupings of those many texts around individual aspects of the Spirit, and these I found useful.

At the same time I must acknowledge the many before me who have analyzed academically several other translations in achieving their individual purposes in writing.

I am grateful (posthumously) to Lloyd Neve who found in 1972 that there was no English language book about the Spirit in the Old Testament and wrote *The Spirit of God in the Old Testament*. He examined texts from each of four chronological periods in order to draw conclusions regarding the concept of Spirit in each period.

Jurgen Moltmann's *The Source of Life* (1997), treating of the Holy Spirit and the theology of life is a classic.

Likewise, in 1998 Leon Wood in his *The Holy Spirit in the Old Testament* found that books about the Holy Spirit considered the subject almost exclusively as a New Testament presentation. His purpose was to present definite things regarding the Holy Spirit and his activity during the Old Testament years.

In 2007 Christopher Wright bemoaned the widespread lack of awareness the identity and impact of the Spirit of God in the bible in the centuries before Christ. The purpose of his *Knowing the Holy Spirit Through the Old Testament* was to ask and answer if we really know the one from whom we expect to receive the sanctity and gifts of the Holy Spirit which was laid out clearly in the Old Testament.

My many allusions to the development of St Augustine's Holy Spirit can be further studied in two wonderful references: *Augustine on the Christian Life: Transformed by the Power of God* by Gerald Bray; and *The Spirit of Augustine's Early Theology* by Chad Tyler Gerber, 2012

A final important resource for me was Stanley Horton's 2005 revised edition of *What the Bible Says About the Holy Spirit*, which follows the Spirit's promise of a Messiah to its fruition in the life of Jesus and his disciples. His stated purpose was simply to go through the bible, book by book, and take a fresh look at what it teaches about the Holy Spirit and his work.

ACKNOWLEDGMENT

Scripture texts in this work are taken from the *New American Bible with Revised New Testament and Psalms* © 1991, 1986, 1970 Confraternity of Christian Doctrine, Washington, D.C. and are used by permission of the copyright owner. All Rights Reserved. No part of the New American Bible may be reproduced in any form without permission in writing from the copyright owner.

Excerpts from the Catechism of the Catholic Church, second edition, copyright © 2000, Libreria Editrice Vaticana-United States Conference of Catholic Bishops, Washington, D.C. Used with permission. All rights reserved.

FOREWORD

I Believe in The Holy Spirit? is a product of Dr. Deegan's exhaustive research into the third person of the Holy Trinity. A clearer understanding of the nature of the Holy Spirit is gained through the author's vast knowledge and use of his resources, namely, the Holy Scriptures (NT) and biblical writings (OT).

Supplemented by utilizing the Catechism of the Catholic Church, decrees of the ecumenical councils, papal encyclicals, classical writings of the saints, and works of various authors in our modern times, Dr. Deegan facilitates the development of a solid foundation and knowledge of the subject.

In the process the reader is drawn into a closer loving relationship with the Holy Spirit. Throughout the book, his statements, commentaries and reflections are complemented by the writings, works and prayers of St. Augustine.

The author's spirituality, grounded in authoritative, sound Catholic teaching and theology, seasons this work with the right amount of his personal experiences, thoughts, reflections and prayers by sharing the intimacy of his own devotion and love of the Holy Spirit.

This, the fourth offering of his books emphasizing spiritual development, focuses on helping the reader to surrender himself to the ultimate goal: STRIVING FOR HOLINESS!

Deacon Gregory Poole
Diocese of Lansing, Michigan
Easter Sunday, 2019

WHAT DOES THE HOLY SPIRIT DO?

I Believe in the Holy Spirit? Why the question mark? When in both the Nicene Creed and the Apostles's Creed we say "...I believe in the Holy Spirit..." just what is it we believe about him? Who is he? What are his attributes? What does he do? These two creeds are given to us as collections of spiritual truths to which we give assent by saying "I believe..." What is a belief? Something we confess to be true, not because we can demonstrate its truth, but on the word of someone else. The words in our creeds are essentially a list of mysteries that we accept on the word of God. It should not surprise us then, that our belief in the Holy Spirit is a little befuddled. Some will think the Father and the Son are important, and the Spirit kind of secondary. But our belief is that they are equal and work in harmony with each other. The uniqueness of the Holy Spirit is His presence within us. Jesus said before he ascended to heaven that the Holy Spirit would come and dwell within us as believers.

On the day of Pentecost, St Peter told the Jewish people to repent of their part in the crucifixion of Jesus and to be baptized in the name of Jesus and they would receive the gift of the Holy Spirit. His must have been a very persuasive promise, for we are told that about three thousand people were added to the Church that day. (cf. Acts 2:41) With that, He empowers us to live victoriously for the cause of Christ and glory of the Father. So one thought comes through loud and clear; namely, that there is a third person in God called the Holy Spirit. But what is his role?

Pope Benedict XVI said it most clearly when he addressed our young on the vigil of World Youth Day in Sydney, Australia, in July 2008. "The Holy Spirit" said the Pontiff, "has in some ways been the neglected person of the Blessed Trinity. ... A clear understanding of the Spirit almost seems beyond our reach."

God the Father seems to be easily envisioned as the Creator, as the God of the Our Father, as the ruler of the universe who will demand an accounting from each of us at the end of time. We have succeeded, with the help of poets and artists to anthropomorphize the Father into a semblance of someone's loving grandfather.

The Son too, who literally shared our humanity, is rather easy to picture as a beautiful infant who grew up to be an itinerant preacher, who ended up suffering a horrible passion and death as our Redeemer. The crucifix we hang around our neck, even the full of mystery Host we adore in our tabernacles and touch with our hands in the Eucharist permit our senses to come to some kind of "understanding" of the second person of the Trinity.

But the Holy Spirit? We tend to give up after drawing a picture of a dove or by saying "No wonder we used to call him the Holy Ghost." So some will simply act as if the Father and Son are enough. It's time to stop such a giving-up attitude about getting to know the Spirit better. Might we begin by undertaking to ascertain more clearly what are the "functions" of the Holy Spirit? What does he do for us and to us? We might call this the role of the Holy Spirit, making allowance for the fact that all such terms cannot really apply to God.

Why search for such a role? For one thing, the Spirit does not speak about himself. He speaks through the prophets to tell us about the Word of the Father. He foretells much about the Son of God who will be our Savior; he describes what we must do to prepare ourselves to welcome the Messiah in faith. But he does not state clearly what his role is. The catechism refers to this as "such properly divine self-effacement". (Catechism of the Catholic Church or CCC, 687) We must watch his actions in sacred scripture and infer from what we see what his proper role is.

Let's return to those two creeds. In the Apostles Creed there is nothing further than the bold statement "I believe in the Holy Spirit," and then we say we believe in other mysteries as well. No help there.

The Nicene Creed is a little more helpful. "I believe in one Lord, Jesus Christ, ... by the Holy Spirit was incarnate of the Virgin Mary, and became man." This is the first mention of the Spirit. It's a good beginning, for it enables us to accept on faith several important truths. Jesus is the Christ; Jesus was born of a virgin; the Spirit was the source of life of the God-man, Jesus. Now I can say that the Spirit I believe in made it possible for Jesus to become man and save my soul. That's a lot!

But there is more: "I believe in the Holy Spirit, the Lord, the giver of life, who proceeds from the Father and the Son, who with the Father and the Son is adored and glorified, who has spoken through the prophets." Here I am saying that I believe that this same Holy Spirit is God (my Lord), and that he is the source of all life. I also believe he is the refulgence of the Father and Son and their love for each other. I believe he is God on a par with the Father and the Son, who is to be adored and glorified. I do not understand all these three names for God, but I believe in this triune God on the word of others. And I believe that it was this same Spirit who used the prophets to speak to us.

Again, that is a lot at least as regards who the Spirit is, but not much about what he does. We must look to other resources. Our catechism is a compendium of what the Church teaches us about our faith (dogmatic theology) and our lives (moral theology). The so-called Baltimore (or "penny") catechism was of a size and structure as to permit our young people to memorize answers to questions. The current catechism (CCC) is more of a research resource, necessarily becoming a challenging tome. Among other things, it explains much more in detail what the creeds tell us about the Holy Spirit. Given that in this book we are attempting to identify a list of "functions" or the role of the Spirit, the CCC provides a lot to develop such a list.

Taken from the chapter on the Holy Spirit, the list might look like this, in shorthand: The Holy Spirit:
- animates all creation
- awakens faith
- enables communication with Christ
- grants gifts to all
- helps us to grow in spiritual freedom
- authors holy scripture
- reveals God/Trinity
- confers all holiness
- unites the Church
- directs and supports the Church

Now, that is a bunch of things I believe in about the Holy Spirit. Which doesn't necessarily mean I understand all these words yet, but it does make this Spirit begin to come alive as a Person who has done some wonderful things. That's a great start.

But as Pope Francis said in one of his homilies: what we have learned and studied in the catechism is not enough to know Jesus. We come to know him as disciples; we come to know him through the daily encounter with the Lord. This is a work of the Holy Spirit, who is a great worker. And he is always at work in us. And he carries out this great work of explaining the mystery of Jesus, and of giving us the mind of Christ. (Paraphrased from a homily of Pope Francis; cf. *Magnificat*, August, 2017, p 389)

Ever since the Councils of Nicea (325) and Constantinople (381) which declared the three person God as an article of faith, we can point to numerous scripture passages that identify all three. When Jesus took leave of his apostles at his ascension to the Father, he gave them their marching orders, instructing them to baptize: "...in the name of the Father and of the Son and of the holy Spirit." (Mt. 28:17) Three persons were also identified by St. Paul often; for example in 2 Cor.13:13: "The grace of the Lord Jesus Christ and the love of God and the fellowship of the holy Spirit be with all of you." So important are they that these are the words that are often used by the presider to begin the Eucharistic liturgy. We also read in 1 Pet. 1:2 "In the foreknowledge of God the Father, through sanctification by the Spirit, for obedience and sprinkling with the blood of Jesus Christ: may grace and peace be yours in abundance."

When we attest our belief in three Persons, we are not talking about parts of God, for he has no parts, He is one. He is indivisible. God sent his Son, the Word, and when the Word became flesh, he did not cease to be the second Person of the Blessed Trinity; he retained his divine nature along with his new (created) human nature. This we believe, though we know not how this can be by human reasoning. Fortunately the Father sent the Spirit along with the Son so he can reveal the Son to us. (cf. CCC, 689)

None of these passages is from the Old Testament. It has been suggested that there is good reason for the Holy Spirit not being recognized as a separate person before the time of Christ.

The Catechism of the Catholic Church sheds some light on this inequality of understanding in paragraph 684: "But The Spirit is the last of the persons of the Holy Trinity to be revealed. St. Gregory of Nazianzus, the Theologian, explains this progression in terms of the pedagogy of Divine "condescension".

He tells us that "the Old Testament proclaimed the Father clearly, but the Son only obscurely. The New Testament revealed the Son and gave but a glimpse of the divinity of the Spirit. Now the Spirit dwells among us and grants us a clearer vision of himself. It was not prudent, when the divinity of the Father had not yet been confessed, to proclaim the Son openly and, when the divinity of the Son was not yet admitted, to add the Holy Spirit as an extra mystery. By advancing and progressing 'from glory to glory' the light of the Trinity can shine in ever more brilliant rays." (St. Gregory Nazianzus, *Oratio theol.*,5,26 [=*Oratio*, 31, 26]: PG 36,161-163)

This book is not really about the Trinity. But the closest expression of our belief about the Holy Spirit is to be found in our theology of the Trinity, especially that articulated by the Doctor of Grace, Saint Augustine, after the definition of the Trinity as an article of Faith.

Discussions of the Trinity observed by the author invariably involve a sense of bewilderment not only about the concept in toto — after all, the Trinity is a mystery — but particularly when it comes to discussing what people before Christ knew or said about the Holy Spirit. Yet what the New Testament writers, and Jesus himself, tell us about the Holy Spirit comes basically from these former adherents to a belief in the Spirit.

Coming to our present age, at the conclusion of Vatican Council II, with its modernization of Christology and particularly the ecclesiology of the Council, the Holy Father called for a new study of, and devotion to, the Holy Spirit as a way to complement the teaching of the Council. (cf General Audience of June 6, 1973: Insegnamenti di Paolo VI, XI, 1973, 477)

Back to Pope Benedict. He said about himself that he must have learned about the Holy Spirit as a young boy, but never quite understood the third person of the Trinity until he was a priest and studied the writings of St. Augustine. Augustine was bishop of Hippo in North Africa in the late 4th and early 5th century. Many think no one had a greater impact on Christian beliefs and practices. Augustine confessed his own understanding of the Holy Spirit "evolved gradually" and was "a struggle". It took some 30 years of wrestling with the concept before he wrote the most famous of his works *De Trinitate* (about the Trinity) around 419 A.D.

Augustine's earlier work, his *Confessions*, was really 13 books, nine of which were autobiographical, the remaining four being commentary. It is not a complete autobiography, as it was written during his early 40's and he lived long afterwards, producing another stellar work, *City of God*. Still, it is almost a chronological record of the development of Augustine's thought, and is a masterful theological text, featuring spiritual meditations and insights. Some see it as divisible into books which symbolize various aspects of the Trinity.

Permit a brief digression that may help appreciate the long time it took for Augustine to complete his study of the Trinity and the Holy Spirit.

Vision of St Augustine by Botticelli

There is a story of an incident when Augustine was walking by the seashore one day contemplating and trying to understand the mystery of the Holy Trinity when he saw a small boy running back and forth from the water to a spot on the seashore. The boy was using a sea shell to carry the water from the ocean and place it into a small hole in the sand.

The Bishop of Hippo approached him and asked, "My boy, what are doing?"

I Believe in the Holy Spirit?

"I am trying to bring all the sea into this hole," the boy replied with a sweet smile.

"But that is impossible, my dear child, the hole cannot contain all that water" said Augustine.

The boy paused in his work, stood up, looked into the eyes of the Saint, and replied, "It is no more impossible than what you are trying to do – comprehend the immensity of the mystery of the Holy Trinity with your small intelligence."

The Saint was absorbed by such a keen response from that child, and turned his eyes from him for a short while. When he glanced down to ask him something else, the boy had vanished.

Some say that it was an Angel sent by God to teach Augustine a lesson on pride in learning. Others affirm it was the Christ Child Himself who appeared to the Saint to remind him of the limits of human understanding the great mysteries of our Faith. May this be a lesson for us also as we plunge ahead to try to understand better the role of the Holy Spirit.

Through this story, the sea shell has become a symbol of St. Augustine and the study of theology.

We shall return to Augustine and the Trinity off and on in explaining several of the Spirit's concepts. But, once again, this is not a book about the Trinity. What we hope to develop is a profile of the work and attributes of the Holy Spirit. Lest I mislead anyone, I must state clearly that my search for his role, for the attributes of the Holy Sprit is a poor metaphor. The Holy

Spirit is the third Person of the Blessed Trinity. He is God. And God is not distinguishable from his attributes. He does not "have" them. He "is" them: He is power, glory, love, mercy. He is one and whole and simple, not made up of any parts. So our search is really for other names for him when we use the term "attributes". The purpose of our search for the role of the third Person of God is simply an attempt to identify and clarify those aspects of God which seem to be apparent in speaking of the third Person, as opposed to the aspects typically associated with the Father and/or the Son.

It is a difficult task we undertake because unlike the Father who spoke directly to Moses in the burning bush, and to the followers of Jesus at his baptism and his transfiguration; and unlike the Son whose many words have been recorded by the evangelists, the Spirit "will not speak on his own." (Jn. 16:13) Still, he has done much and said much through others which can help us in our attempt to develop this role. Obviously we cannot rely on a supernatural vision or apparition to flesh out this third Person of the Blessed Trinity. Our resource must be the same as for all our religious beliefs, namely the bible.

Spirit versus Holy Spirit

The reader will note that the term used in the Old Testament over 200 times is "Spirit". Only three times do we find him called the "Holy Spirit" in the Hebrew bible. In Psalm 51, called the miserere or prayer of repentance, verse 13 says:

> "Do not drive me from your presence,
> nor take from me your holy spirit."

Two-times in Isaiah, the unfaithfulness of the chosen people is said to displease the holy Spirit:

> "But they rebelled, and grieved his holy spirit;
> So he turned on them like an enemy,
> and fought against them," (Is 63:10)

and

> "Then they remembered the days of old
> and Moses, his servant;
> Where is he who brought up out of the sea
> the shepherd of his flock?
> Where is he who put his holy spirit
> in their midst?" (Is 63:11)

There is no discernible reason for adding the adjective holy in these instances compared to all the other uses of the simple term Spirit.

Another place in some translations of the Old Testament where the Holy Spirit is mentioned by name is in the introductory verses of the book of Sirach which extolled wisdom as coming from the Lord and having been created before all things else. As the last of the Books of Wisdom, Sirach contains many maxims dealing with faith and morals. Its author, about 200 years before the birth of Christ, wrote to help his contemporaries maintain their faith through study of the holy books and tradition. Since that is exactly the approach taken by the followers of Christ, it is not surprising that this book was used extensively by the Church in presenting moral teaching to catechumens and the faithful. Teaching is one of the works of the Holy Spirit who speaks to us through the inspired words of scripture.

Sirach says only the Lord fully understands wisdom, so that the beginning of wisdom for us is fear of the Lord. We all aspire to have wisdom, which is listed as one of the gifts of the Holy Spirit. It is helpful to know that "It is the Lord; he created her" (Sir 1:7) through the holy Spirit. The Hebrews did not speak of the spirit or holy Spirit as one person out of three in the Trinity, for these concepts were not developed until the Christian era. For them the term is synonymous with the presence of God within an individual or the chosen people as a whole.

Holy Spirit versus Holy Ghost

Many Christians were raised to bless themselves "In the name of the Father and the Son and the Holy Ghost." This was the accepted name for the third person of the Trinity. Why the change to Spirit? Where did the term *ghost* come from? Legionary of Christ Father Edward McNamara, professor of liturgy at the Regina Apostolorum University in Rome explains as follows. The change from *ghost* to *spirit* reflects the evolution of the words. Both were used to refer to the Third Person well before the 20th century. The word *ghost* is of Germanic origin and comes from the Old English *gast*, meaning soul, life, breath, good or bad spirit, angel or demon. Christian texts in Old English use *gast* to translate the Latin *spiritus* from where we get Holy Ghost. Consider that the word *gast* sneaked into our word *aghast* meaning to be terrified, shocked or rendered breathless. The more modern understanding of ghost to be a disembodied dead person gradually seemed inappropriate to refer to God. Spirit, on the other hand, comes to English from the Latin through French and also means soul, courage, vigor, breath — all words more fitting for the third Person.

In a word, the change was not a decree from Vatican II or other Church command, but we will always refer to Spirit or Holy Sprit as "he"and not "it". This is because his will and knowledge and love reveal his personhood and not merely an impersonal force or symbol of God's power.

We will be citing many places in both the Old and New Testaments in searching for a more concrete appreciation for the work of the Holy Spirit. We will see that a list of what he did before the birth of Christ would compare very closely with his work in the Christian era. For the Spirit was foretold to bring salvation not only to the Jewish people but also to the Gentiles as can be seen in Joel 3:1 referring to "all mankind", Haggai 2:7 with reference to "all the nations" and Isaiah 66:18 to "nations of every language".

We could make a brief list from the words of Jesus himself in his Last Supper discourse. The Spirit/Advocate will comfort (Jn 14:16); he will promote truth (Jn 14:17); he will teach (Jn 14:26); he will give witness (testify) about Jesus (Jn 14:26); he will convict of sin (Jn 16:8) he will emphasize righteousness (Jn 16:10); he will glorify Jesus (Jn 16: 14); he will communicate Christ's word (Jn 16:15). But all of these come with no further explanation.

Having found a beginning place, we now need additional help in making that list of things the Spirit does become more real, more visible, so to speak. We could go to the infallible teachers of our modern church, the recent Roman Pontiffs. In recent years there have been three encyclicals about the Holy Spirit: 1) Leo XIII, who published the Encyclical Epistle *Divinum Illud Munus* (1897); 2) Pius XII, who wrote the encyclical letter *Mystici Corporis* (1943); and John Paul 11 who gave us *Dominum et Vivificantem*, On the Holy Spirit in the Life of the Church and the World (1986). All three of these are beautiful, theological explanations of the Holy Spirit and his work for the Triune God. Excellent references for the reader, but far more weighty than desired for our simple attempt to identify the functions of the Spirit in this volume.

We might mention, however, that when Pope St John Paul II wrote his encyclical he said its purpose was to fulfill the duty of the "Church... compelled by the Holy Spirit to do her part towards the full realization of the will of God". The Spirit's role, therefore, is to speak through the Church to see that the will of God is carried out. There is a beginning of identifying one function of the Holy Spirit.

To be guided in our search by a somewhat less "deep" resource, let us turn our attention, then, to another work of Saint Augustine, his very brief Prayer to the Holy Spirit for the help we need. Having confessed his earlier life of sin and self-centeredness, he decided it was time for him to heed the words of God "Be holy, for I... am holy." (Dt 6:4; Lev 19:2) Believing strongly that the Spirit is the source of grace, defined as a state of holiness, he penned the following prayer:

> Breathe in me, O Holy Spirit,
> > that my thoughts may all be holy.
> Move in me, O Holy Spirit,
> > that my words, too, may be holy.
> Attract my heart, O Holy Spirit,
> > that I may love only what is holy.
> Strengthen me, O Holy Spirit,
> > that I may defend all that is holy.
> Protect me then, O Holy Spirit
> > that I always may be holy. Amen.

There are five different requests in this prayer and one overriding theme. Each verse seems to focus on one or other of the main features of the Spirit, while the overriding theme is the desire to be holy, as the reason for being created. The purpose of this book is to develop the role of the Holy Spirit - a description of what he has been doing vis-a-vis the human race from the foundation of the world. If Saint Augustine saw these as fruits to be asked of the Holy Spirit, perhaps they can serve us as a framework for culling from the words of scripture, and from all we study in the CCC, our sought for role. We might daringly call them "functions", "marks" or "attributes" of the

Holy Spirit. They then become the subject of the chapters that follow.

Author's Note

At the conclusion of each chapter you will find a Brief Conversation with the Holy Spirit. This is in the belief that the best way to develop any relationship is one-on-one conversation. And while I will write words in this conversation, the real point is that I must spend some time in the presence of the Holy Spirit (conversation meaning coming together) if I am going to learn anything at all about him. The work preparing this text is primarily to help deepen my own personal relationship with the Paraclete. You will also find from time to time throughout this volume that I offer a question or comment to you in the second person. This is an effort to get closer to you in our discussion about this important topic.

THE HOLY SPIRIT AS BREATH OF LIFE

Breathe into me, O Holy Spirit,
That my thoughts may all be holy.

This mention of the Spirit by Saint Augustine as one who breathes is perhaps indicative of the most exalted of the attributes of the Holy Spirit. This verse is a plea for the breath of continued life, or constant renewal, or the indwelling of the source of grace. In terms of the work of the Spirit, we believe that:

He creates life
He gives right order
He causes rebirth
He baptizes
He can end life

He creates life

The power of the Spirit to give life is stated most explicitly in the first chapter St. Luke's gospel, the passage about the Annunciation and Incarnation of Jesus. When Mary asks the Archangel Gabriel how she could possibly give life to a son, she is told:
"The holy Spirit will come upon you, and the power of the Most High will overshadow you ..." (Lk. 1:35) It is the Holy Spirit who gave life to Jesus in the womb of Mary. The Spirit who overshadowed Mary in the New Testament was hovering over the Lord's newly created world in a way compared later (in Dt 32:11) to the eagle fluttering over its brood.

New Testament citations are very explicit in attributing life-giving power to the Holy Spirit. Nowhere is this more direct than in the beginning of Matthew's gospel when he shows that the Spirit was behind the life of Jesus: "Now this is how the birth of Jesus Christ came about. When his mother Mary was betrothed to Joseph, but before they lived together, she was found with child through the holy Spirit." (Mt 1:18) And again in Mt. 1:20 "Such was his intention when, behold, the angel of the Lord appeared to him in a dream and said, "Joseph, son of David, do not be afraid to take Mary your wife into your home. For it is through the holy Spirit that this child has been conceived in her." Or in Luke 1:35 "And the angel said to her in reply 'The holy Spirit will come upon you, and the power of the Most High will overshadow you. Therefore the child to be born will be called holy, the Son of God.' "

But before that, time after time in sacred scripture that breath of God gives life. It began when this Spirit brought order out of chaos in the first act of creation. Hovering over the early darkness that encompassed our world, the Spirit responded to the various thoughts of God beginning with "...let there be..." and made it so. Whether it was day and night, the teeming sea, the mountains and landmasses, or the stars of the sky, the Spirit was God's creative action. So when it came to the birds of the air, the fish in the sea, the beasts of the forest, or humans to rule over them as living creatures, the Spirit breathed life into them all.

The work of creation by the Father refers to the primordial waters which were made out of nothing by God. "The earth was a formless wasteland, and darkness covered the abyss." (Gen 1:2) But "a mighty wind swept over the waters." (Gen 1:2) That wind was the Spirit. Under his power God then continued his work of creation. It was the work of the Holy Spirit to bring things to life and to set things in order. He brought forth light out of darkness and order out of disorder. Thus, part of the first "function" of the Holy Spirit, as breather of life is also to set things in order.

"He is not the God of disorder, but of peace." (1 Cor 14:33) We do not know how all that took place, but we are sure that it did. "By faith we understand that the universe was ordered by the word of God, so that what is visible came into being through the invisible." (Heb 11:3)

The ancient hymn *Veni Creator Spiritus*, composed in the eighth century and part of the Roman breviary of Vespers, is a hymn extolling the Holy Spirit. John Dryden's magnificent translation renders the opening lines this way: "Creator Spirit, by whose aid the world's foundations first were laid..." This indicates the tradition in the Church that the Holy Spirit had a part in the creation story.

It begins in Genesis 1:2 where we read "the earth was a formless wasteland, and darkness covered the abyss, while a mighty wind swept over the waters." The interesting part of this is the Hebrew word for spirit. Our translation uses the word "wind" for the Hebrew "ruach". Scholars point out the many other possible meanings in different circumstances. It means "air in motion." It is the same word for "breath." It also means "life." By resemblance to breath and air in motion, it means "spirit". That's where some get their translation in this Genesis verse, for the Hebrew word contains all those different meanings: they are all invisible, untouchable and formless. David was sure that this was the meaning of the creation story, for he wrote:

> "By the LORD's word the heavens were made;
> by the breath of his mouth all their host." (Ps 33:6)

Then when God created Adam, he "formed man out of the clay of the ground and blew into his nostrils the breath of life, and so man became a living being." (Gen 2:7)

That location for the gift of life to enter a human body was a vivid image for generations in the Old Testament, Thus we find Job, despite his many misfortunes, saying

> "So long as I still have life in me
> and the breath of God is in my nostrils. . ." (Job 27:3)

Later, Elihu angrily remonstrates Job, his elder, and says

> "For the spirit of God has made me,
> the breath of the Almighty keeps me alive."
> (Job 33:4)

This life-giving attribute of the Spirit was so understood by the people of the Old Testament that we find Ezekiel's well known vision of the dry bones, when the people of Israel had just about given up hope. The spirit of the Lord set this prophet in the middle of a plain in which he saw countless dry (lifeless) bones, referred to as the "whole house of Israel". He was commanded by the Lord: "Prophesy to the spirit, prophesy, son of Man, and say to the spirit: ... From the four winds come, O spirit, and breathe into these slain that they may come to life." (Ez 37:9) And, of course, Ezekiel did as he was commanded, "... and the spirit came into them; they came alive and stood upright, a vast army." (Ez 37:10)

The prophet Job — he whose family and material goods were taken from him as a test of his devotion and belief in God — is very clear about indicating the Spirit is the source of life. Job 33:4 says

> "The Spirit of God has made me,
> and the breath of the Almighty keeps me alive".

He also attests to the Spirit sustaining that life, as in Job 27:3

> "So long as I still have life in me
> and the breath of God is in my nostrils…".

It is the same Spirit that breathes initial life and sustains that life:

> "For the spirit of God has made me,
> the breath of the Almighty keeps me alive."
> (Job 33:4)

And finally Job, aware of how much God can take back, identifies the Spirit breath as the actor in removing life:

> "If he were to take back his spirit to himself,
> withdraw to himself his breath…" (Job 34:14)

These and other places in the Old Testament indicate belief in the Spirit; but did the people of that time see the spirit as power and source of life, and as a divine Person, the third person of the Trinity? Probably not, since that terminology was not the accepted theology until the Council of Nicea over three centuries after the birth of Christ. As we saw earlier, only three times in the Old Testament is he spoken of as the <u>Holy</u> Spirit.

We should not be concerned about the various names for him. He is sometimes called the Spirit of God (Gen 1:2) and at other times the Spirit of Jahweh (Judges 3:10). The latter seems to be a more intimate name, referring to God's contact with humankind. In the New Testament he will be called the Paraclete or Advocate or Consoler (about which we will have much to say later). Jesus at the last Supper called him "the Spirit of truth." (Jn16:13) St Paul will then use a variety of titles, such as the Spirit of the promise, the Spirit of adoption, the Spirit of Christ, the

Spirit of the Lord and the Spirit of God, while St Peter will refer to the Spirit of Glory.

He gives right order

Right order is the harmony that exists when all things are in their proper relationship with God. "In the beginning when God created the heavens and the earth, the earth was a formless wasteland, and darkness covered the abyss..." (Gen 1:1-2) One imagines a sight of total chaos, the absence of order, pitch black depths with no symmetry. But then we are told in the last phrase of that same verse, "... while a mighty wind swept over the waters." We have seen that the word "wind" refers to the Holy Spirit. God then, one by one, exercised his creative power and made day and night, the sky and stars in the sky, the sun and the moon, seas and dry land, plants and trees, fishes and birds, animals and humans. The power of God that made this happen in a way that set up proper relationships with God was that wind or Spirit.

To those who think the world and all that is in it could have just developed by itself in right order, someone used an analogy. What are the odds of shuffling a deck of cards and having them wind up in the correct order they had when you first opened that deck? That is, two to ace, spades, hearts, diamonds and clubs. The odds are about 1 in 10 to the power of 68 (or 1 followed by 68 zeros), said to be roughly the number of atoms in our galaxy.

When God completed his creation, he saw that it was all good and there was peace on earth. St. Augustine says peace is the tranquility of order. When Adam and Eve sinned, they disturbed God's right oder by wanting to be gods themselves at the suggestion of Satan. This destroyed their relationship with God so much that it would not be restored until the Son of God himself ransomed us by his passion and death on the Cross.

When you receive the Holy Spirit through baptism, he makes Jesus Christ the center of your life. Everything in your life is brought into the proper relationship with God. You are at peace. "Peace I leave with you; my peace I give to you." (Jn 14:27) Should you become unfaithful to your baptismal vows, you will quickly sense the disorder in your life, the lack of peace, the need for restoring right order. You have only to turn to the Holy Spirit and pray: "Come, Holy Spirit, fill my heart with your love, and enkindle in me the fire of that love." He is waiting for your call to restore order and peace. The disorder in your life was caused by replacing the will of God with allegiance to your own will. To restore order you have just to say with Jesus in the Garden of Gethsemane "Not my will, but yours be done." The right order of things is life arranged with God and his will at the center and everything else arrayed in proper (subservient) relationship with that will.

All of the disorder in our world can be explained by the fact that it has disordered the relationship with Christ and his Church: social disorder, political disorder, economic disorder, moral disorder. There is no right order in world affairs today. When God is not welcome in our schools, our courts, our government halls, our places of work, our bedrooms, there is no right order. St Paul describes restoring right order: "For just as in Adam all die, so too in Christ shall all be brought to life, but each one in proper order: Christ the firstfruits; then, at his coming, those who belong to Christ; then comes the end, when he hands over the kingdom to his God and Father, when he has destroyed every sovereignty and every authority and power." (1Cor 15:22-24)

This refers to the end times, as envisioned in the Book of Revelation, chapter 20, when the day will come for Jesus to be recognized as King. There will be a period of peace on earth once again, to last for one thousand years. The Holy Spirit will once again hover over all creation awaiting the second coming. We anticipate those days as our rightful inheritance after living a life in company with the Holy Spirit, and so we pray in many opening prayers at Mass that believers in Christ will rise through the Holy Spirit to eternal life. This has been the song of glory of all the saints before us. Listen to the final words of St. Polycarp as he won his martyr's crown, preferring the pain of burning to death rather than abjuring his faith in Jesus:

"God of angels, of powers, of all creation, of all the race of saints who live in your sight, I bless you for judging me worthy of this day, of this hour, so that in the company of the martyrs I may share the cup of Christ, your anointed one, and so rise again to eternal life in soul and body, immortal through the power of the Holy Spirit." (cited in *Patrology*, Vol One, *The Beginnings of Patristic Literature*)

He causes rebirth

The phrase "born again" first appears in the gospel of John. when Jesus startled Nicodemus, a learned Pharisee and new believer in the works of Jesus: "Amen, amen, I say to you, no one can see the kingdom of God without being born from above." (Jn 3:3) When Nicodemus asked him how this could be done, the Lord told him: "What is born of flesh is flesh and what is born of the spirit is spirit. Do not be amazed that I told you, 'You must be born from above.' The wind blows where it wills, and you can hear the sound it makes, but you do not know where it comes from or where it goes; so it is with everyone who is born of the Spirit." (Jn 3:6-8) It is the Spirit then who gives this new birth, one of spiritual life.

Jesus is talking about the Holy Spirit, and He is saying it is like wind. The Greek word is "pneuma", which again means "a current of air," "breath," or a "breeze," and again by analogy, "a spirit." So both the Hebrew and the Greek word are talking about breath, talking about wind, talking about a spirit. As a matter of fact, that is one of the distinguishing marks of the Jewish religion. No other nation in the ancient Near East attributed a spirit to its gods; only the Jews who adored only one God had this unique way of referring to their God.

At times, the wind itself is symbolically used in scripture to indicate the action of the Spirit. Most significant of these is the passage in Acts describing the descent of the Holy Spirit on the apostles. "When the time for Pentecost was fulfilled, they were all in one place together. And suddenly there came from the sky a noise like a strong driving wind, and it filled the entire house in which they were." (Acts 1:1-2)

This is the fulfillment of the promise Jesus made to send the Spirit upon the Apostles. We say they were "reborn" by that new indwelling of the Spirit within them. We can speak then of the Holy Spirit being the source of life and also of a new life or "rebirth". He generates life and regenerates it. Ezekiel had referenced regeneration when he prophesied: "I will give them a new heart and put a new spirit within them; I will remove the stony heart from their bodies, and replace it with a natural heart" (Ez 11:19); and again in Ez 36:26-27, "I will give you a new heart, and place a new spirit within you, taking from your bodies your stony hearts and giving you natural hearts. I will put my spirit within you...".

It should be clear from these quotations that being reborn is not to be taken literally as regards our human bodies, as even Nicodemus scoffingly said to Jesus: "Surely he [a person] cannot renter his mother's womb and be born again, can he?" (Jn 3:4) The answer given by Jesus suggests that a person will not necessarily see the rebirth take place. "The wind blows where it wills, and you can hear the sound it makes, but you do not know where it comes from or where it goes; so it is with everyone who is born of the Sport." (Jn 3:8)

When we are re-born, then, it is from that same breath of God. Jesus made this evident when he first appeared to the apostles after his resurrection. "Peace be with you", he said, "As the Father has sent me, so I send you." And when he had said this, he breathed on them and said to them, "Receive the holy Spirit. ..." (Jn 20:21-22) Just as God breathed human life into Adam, Jesus is breathing spiritual life into the apostles.

The close relationship between "breath" and "spirit" as translations of the same Hebrew word suggests that if a person has breath he is alive physically, and if he has the Spirit of God, he is alive spiritually. Another comment by Augustine will be helpful to start us on the right path to being reborn. He said: "Nobody can be born of the Spirit without being humble, because humility is what brings us to birth by the Spirit, because the Lord is close to those whose hearts are bruised." (cf. *Homilies on John*, 12, 233)

What kind of life results from this second birth?

Since it is not to be reserved for only a favored few, but to be available to everyone it must be something understandable for the common person. Jeremiah prophesied about this spiritual new birth by the Holy Spirit as part of the new covenant God would make with his people: "It will not be like the covenant I made with their fathers... I will place my law within them, and write it upon their hearts; I will be their God, and they shall be my people" (Jer 31: 32-33) Or as Ezekiel later put it: "I will give them a new heart and put a new spirit within them; I will remove the stony heart from their bodies, and replace it with a natural heart, so that they will live according to my statutes." (Ez 11: 19-20)

At the other end of the Bible, the book of Revelation depicts the "(seven) spirits" that are "sent out into the whole world" (Rev 5:6); they are symbolic of the Holy Spirit as the one again waiting to carry out the wishes of God. In order to deal with the degradation of an evil age, the Spirit has intensified himself seven times to help us to overcome and not be fashioned according to evil. The hovering Spirit who watched over the formless creation now broods over the cosmos, seeking to bring about a new creation, thereby ensuring its formation according to the perfect plan of God. (cf. Derek Thomas "The Breath of God" article in *Tabletalk Magazine*, 7/1/04).

He baptizes

At times the coming of the Holy Spirit is marked by visible signs from God. This is most evident in the case of the apostles at Pentecost when the arrival of the promised Advocate was accompanied by strong winds and flames of fire. This baptism of the Spirit (Mt 3:11, Acts 1:5, and Acts 2:33-4) was repeated on other followers of Jesus as in Acts 11:15-17.

There seems to be two distinct experiences. Jesus is baptized by John in Luke 3:21-22. Then there is an additional coming or deepening of the Spirit in Acts 1:4-5 and Acts 8:14-16. In like manner, an additional blessing by the Spirit is necessary for all Christians because we are all called to some kind of ministry; i.e., to spread the good news of the Gospel. Thus had Joel prophesied:

> "Then afterward I will pour out
> my spirit upon all mankind.
> Your sons and daughters shall prophesy;
> .. Even upon the servants and the handmaids,
> in those days I will pour out my spirit." (Jl 3:1-2)

We say often that Jesus is the Way, the Truth and the Life. Is that taking anything away from the Holy Spirit as the author of all life? Jesus himself explains: "It is the spirit that gives life, while the flesh is of no avail. The words I have spoken to you are spirit and life" (Jn 6:63). It is the words of Jesus that explain how to live a holy life in opposition to one rooted in the pleasures of the flesh. The Spirit creates life, while Jesus is the way or model of how to live that life.

The difference between citations from the Old Testament and those from the New is, of course, that the early Hebrews were not thinking of a distinct Person of God when they referred to the spirit. (Note they did not capitalize the word either.) As a rule, they were thinking of the spirit as God using his energy to accomplish what he wanted done. But from the above citations, it is clear that in both testaments there is a close relationship between "breath" and "spirit" and "wind". We today speak of getting the wind knocked out of us, when referring to a temporary loss of breath. So too when a person stops breathing, we say his spirit has left him.

He can end life

The Jewish people had a concept of obedient death: you hand back to God the breath he gave you.

The life created by the Spirit after the fall of Adam and Eve was not intended to be a permanent condition for that bundle of bones. Which raises the question about man's longevity. Biblical longevity refers to the claimed biologically-impossible life spans of some Biblical characters, which were often hundreds of years long. Some characters in the bible simply live too long (in terms of hundreds of years). In Several books of the Old Testament (Joshua, Job and 2 Chronicles) we read about several individuals with rather long life spans, up to the 969 years attributed to Methusalah. This biological impossibility might be explained by mistranslating the word month for year. That would change Methusalah's 969 years to 78.3 years.

God sent the flood because he was angry over the evil lives of humans. He then declared: "My spirit shall not remain in man forever, since he is but flesh. His days shall comprise one hundred and twenty years." (Gen 6:3) However, in later passages of the Bible there are people who blatantly defy this command and live far more than 120 years. Abraham lived to the ripe old age of 175 years old (with the physical prowess to father a child at 100 years of age!) Abraham's wife Sarah is the only woman in the Old testament whose age is given. She was 127 (Gen 23:1). Noah lived for 950 years (That's longer than Adam!) Moses led the exodus when he was 80 and lived for 40 years in the desert, making nicely the age of precisely 120.

Similar remarkable longevities are put forth in the traditions of Hinduism, Islam, Janism, as well as non-sectarian histories; traditions about long-lived people, either as individuals or groups of people, and practices that have been believed to confer longevity, but for which scientific evidence does not support the ages claimed or the reasons for the claims.

The Spirit not only gives life, but he also can take it away. As his wind blows or breathes life into the world and into humans, so too it can be a destructive force. For example, we read in Exodus (15:10) about the Egyptians perishing in their attempt to prevent the Israelites from fleeing across the Red Sea:

> "When your wind blew, the sea covered them;
> like lead they sank in the mighty waters,"

where wind is again the same breath of God.

David sang after the Lord delivered him from the hands of his enemies and of Saul:

> "Then the wellsprings of the sea appeared;
> the foundations of the earth were laid bare

> At the rebuke of the Lord,
> at the blast of the wind of his wrath." (2 Sam 22:16)

In Job it is quite clear:

> "By the breath of God they perish,
> and by the blast of his wrath they are consumed." (Job 4:9)

His breath can indeed be destructive:

> "He shall strike the ruthless with the rod of his mouth,
> and with the breath of his lips he shall slay the wicked." (Is 11:4)

And again:

> "Scarcely are they planted or sown,
> scarcely is their stem rooted in the earth,
> When he breathes upon them and they wither,
> and the stormwind carries them away like straw."
> (Is 40:24)

And this ending of mortal life can be for multitudes at a single time, as happened at the time of Noah. "When God saw how corrupt the earth had become, since all mortals led depraved lives on earth, he said to Noah: 'I have decided to put an end to all mortals on earth; the earth is full of lawlessness because of them. I will destroy them and all life on earth." (Gen 6:12-13). We know making such judgements is the work of the Holy Spirit, from the words of Jesus: "I will send him to you. And when he comes he will convict the world in regard to sin and righteousness and condemnation...." (Jn 16:7-8)

Conclusion

It would seem that the first "function"of the Holy Spirit is to give and sustain life, or bring it to an end. Psalm 104:30 says

> "When you send forth your breath, they are created; and you renew the face of the earth."

While verse 29 says

> "When you hide your face, they are lost.
> When you take away their breath, they perish and return to the dust from which they came."

The Holy Spirit creates natural life and spiritual life.

It is said that the difference between life of a man and life of an animal is man's power to think: he is a rational animal. That would suggest that thinking is what I do with most of my life. As I acknowledge the Holy Spirit to be the giver of my birth and my rebirth, he must control my thinking. And because he is holiness himself, anything associated with him should also be holy. Because he is the author of my life, I beg him to keep all my thoughts holy, as Augustine does in this first verse of his prayer.

A BRIEF CONVERSATION WITH THE HOLY SPIRIT

Come, O Holy Spirit, and sustain the life you have given me.

> "You formed my inmost being;
> You knit me in my mother's womb.
> I praise you, so wonderfully you made me;
> Wonderful are your works. (Ps 139:13-14)

Most Holy Spirit, I am in awe of your power over life. You are its author; you are its source; you are its custodian. You give it where you will; you withhold it where you will. I have always been taught that life is the most important of all considerations for us humans. Every aspect of our culture begins with reflection on how it might effect life among us. Of all the gifts I must thank my God for, life is first. I therefore come before you on bended knee and profoundly give you thanks for this great gift.

I thank you for permitting me to live in a country where life is so prized, where you are recognized as the giver of that life. At the same time, I am dismayed at the myopic view so many have when they speak of our country's belief in "life, liberty and the pursuit of happiness" since the life of the unborn means so little to them. I beg you to strengthen our belief in the sanctity of life. Please bring an end to abortion, the wantless taking of the life you have placed in the wombs of so many who decide it is not worth anything.

O, the power you have as you bestow life where you will. You have only to breathe gently and life is created. You have only to hover silently like a shadow over something and life is created. You have only to blow as a whispering wind and life is created. The most awesome item in the lexicon of mankind (life) is created by such a simple action on your part! I cannot conceive of any greater power in the universe. Our atom or hydrogen bombs pale in comparison with the result of your willing life to be.

And my reaction to this incomprehensible truth? A realization that it all begins with you! Without life, there is no I. There is no adoration, no thanksgiving, no thought, word or deed on my part, because there is no I. We are at the very beginning of everything, because without your hovering there is only chaos.

Hear my prayer as I paraphrase the third Eucharistic prayer: By your power and work, O Holy Spirit, give life to all things and make them holy; never cease to gather a people to yourself; from the rising of the sun to its setting, may we, with humble spirit, adore and worship you!

Encapsulating all these aspects of the life-giving breath of God, I begin my day with prayer of thanksgiving "You made me, you saved me, you called me, you sustain me - praise to you, O Spirit of God."

But once you deign to turn my dust into a living being, there are so many corollaries that I must address. As toward anyone toward whom I am in debt, I must try to repay it. But, of course, it is impossible to repay you for my life. I can only offer it back to you, and I do by saying "Do with my life what you will".

The question then becomes, What do I do with this precious gift of life? I consecrate it to you and intend to live it wholly at your disposal. I surrender the human will that comes with this life to your divine will, so that I live in your will. Like two streams that become one river, like two drops that become one, like two flames that become a single light, I wish to devote my entire life to your service, so that my will becomes identical with yours.

As I see the fleeting years of my life fall away, I realize how little I have thought of you. Having received the gift of life, I have taken it for granted for so many years. I have proudly thought I was master of my life and failed to recognize I have long lived on borrowed time. For this I am ashamed and plead with you that you overlook this self-centeredness, and continue to breathe fresh life in my tired bones so that my life not be an entire waste of your generosity.

With St. Augustine, I pray: BREATHE INTO ME, O HOLY SPIRIT, SO THAT MY THOUGHTS MAY ALL BE HOLY!

THE HOLY SPIRIT AS INSPIRER

Move in me, O Holy Spirit,
That my words too may be holy.

This request is for wisdom to preach, to inspire others, to prophesize. Here Saint Augustine wants to be sure that he is in tune with the Spirit so that his work would help all to be holy. He echoes the prayer for the Holy Spirit who inspired holiness in the Old Testament believers, "May your kind Spirit guide me on ground that is level." (Psalm 143:10)

Saint Augustine, bishop of Hippo, authored this short prayer knowing he needed that same kind of double inspiration as he presided over his flock and also to refute heresies of his day. He felt his calling was to emulate some of the prophets — not as a predictor of the future, but as a conveyor of the truth of the Lord, which is the essence of prophesying. In terms of the role of the Holy Spirit, we believe that:

> He inspires our thoughts and words
> He gives a new mind
> He helps us understand scripture (which he wrote)
> He inspires prophets
> He inspires in the New Testament
> He gives gifts and fruits
> He teaches us how to pray

He inspires our thoughts and words

Jesus told his disciples not to worry when they are handed over to persecutors: "...do not worry about how you are to speak or what you are to say. You will be given at that moment what you are to say. For it will not be you who speak but the Spirit of your Father speaking through you" (Mt 10: 19-20); and "For the holy Spirit will teach you at that moment what you are to say." (Lk 12:12)

On another occasion, Jesus realized that his followers were getting to the point of overload from his teachings. So he calmed them down by saying: "I have much more to tell you, but you cannot bear it now. But when he comes, the Spirit of truth, he will guide you to all truth..." (Jn16: 12-13) Other translators add: "... and bring to your remembrance all that I said to you." Jesus is speaking here of a special imparting of inspiration from the Holy Spirit. Such divine inspiration is clearly what Augustine sees here as a special gift of the Spirit. The very word inspiration suggests that the spirit will move into a person.

These promises will not be difficult to appreciate, for many of you will have been in a situation when you were not sure what exactly you were going to say, only to find that somehow the right words just came to you. "I was somehow inspired what to say" will be your explanation. Such inspirations come of a sudden, from we know not where, and permit the receiver to speak/write in a manner beyond one's natural capacity.

Such divine guidance (inspiration) may also be given by the Spirit to a group, especially regarding important decisions. When the first followers of Jesus met at the Council of Jerusalem, as recorded in the Acts of the Apostles, especially to resolve the dispute about circumcision for newly baptized Gentiles, we read: "It is the decision of the holy Spirit and of us not to place on you any burden beyond these necessities..." (Acts 15:28)

For this reason it is common practice for decision-making bodies to offer a prayer asking for the guidance (inspiration) of the Holy Spirit in all deliberations. Even civic democratic bodies that believe in separation of church and state somehow feel the need to seek divine guidance publicly before coming to order.

It is also common for individuals who recognize their own limitations in formulating wise thoughts or messages to be prompted by the Spirit to seek inspiration from the bible. Religious services of all denominations include readings and interpretation of passages from the bible as the cornerstone for all teaching in homilies and/or reflections. Which is an implicit recognition that: "All scripture is inspired by God and is useful for teaching, for refutation, for correction, and for training in righteousness." (2 Tim. 3:16) The Holy Spirit is again the source of inspiration.

Those who seek inspiration thus from the bible were warned by St. Peter: "Know this first of all, that there is no prophecy of scripture that is a matter of personal interpretation, for no prophecy ever came through human will; but rather human beings moved by the holy Spirit spoke under the influence of God" (2 Pet. 1:20-21). We can be sure, in other words, that what we read in scripture is not a figment of some one's imagination, but the third Person of the Trinity speaking through human authors, he being the prime author of the holy book. Neither should private interpretation change what was intended to be said by the Holy Spirit when other humans offer the words of scripture for the edification of the people.

He gives a new mind

God is not interested in saving our mortal bodies for all eternity. What does interest him is our mind, our human spirit. Once that is in order, God can supply it with an immortal spirit-infused resurrected body when the strife of earthly living comes to an end.

It behooves us, then, to ask for the renewed mind that St Paul spoke of to the Romans. "Do not conform yourselves to this age but be transformed by the renewal of your mind, that you may discern what is the will of God, what is good and pleasing and perfect." (Rom 12:2) The mind being ethereal, it falls into the domain of the Holy Spirit for proper care and nourishment. The mind possesses a God-given freedom of will. We have the ability to choose from among options as to how we direct our life. In what some call his valedictorian speech, Moses told the people: "I call heaven and earth today to witness against you. I have set before your life and death, the blessing and the curse. Choose life, then, that you and your descendants may live." (Dt 30:19)

How many choices do we make every day? What time to get up? What to wear? What road to take to get to work? What papers or books to read? What TV shows to watch? What kind of friends to have? Even to buy milk at the grocery, we have to choose skim, 1%, 2%, low fat, whole, white, chocolate, or strawberry!

Augustine commented that the punishment of every disordered mind is its own disorder. We can take that to mean that if we rely on our own puny intellect to always make the right choices, we will soon find ourselves lost in a morass of if's and but's and maybe's. We do not in our fallen state have everything in the right order. We are caught on the horns of our own petard, as Shakespeare would say. Recalling that the Holy Spirit creates right order out of chaos, we plead for him to give us a new mind.

The critical question is: by whose guidelines do we make our decisions? We must allow the Holy Spirit to develop the same attitude of Christ in our mind as urged by St Paul: "Have among yourselves the same attitude that is also yours in Christ Jesus" (Phil 2:5) An old (natural) mind might use feelings, prejudices, lusts, peer pressure, political gain or other mortal standards. But the new (spiritual) mind given by the Spirit will help us choose based on God's will.

My mind will be merged with his. "Just like two streams that peacefully come together to form one river, two drops that become just one, and two flames that form a single light; in this way I must forget myself at all times, to make my whole will merge with God's. May I be attentive to his every wish, make me desire only what he desires and long for only what he wants." (From a prayer of Servant of God Louisa Picarreta)

We are asking here, then, for the courage to live a different lifestyle from what the world offers with its behaviors and customs, which are usually selfish and often corrupting. Instead we will choose based on Jesus Christ "who gave himself for our sins that he might rescue us from the present evil age in accord with the will of our God and Father." (Gal. 1:4)

He helps us understand scripture (which he wrote)

The bible is the word of God, specifically the words of the Holy Spirit who wrote through human authors. That word of God is essential for us as the Spirit guides and protects us on our pilgrimage amid the dangers of this world. It was true for our ancestors:

> "Your all-powerful word from heaven's royal throne bounded, fierce warrior, into the doomed land, bearing the sharp sword of your inexorable decree.'" (Wis 18:15-16)

St. Paul told the Ephesians to arm themselves for daily battle against evil: "In all circumstances, hold faith as a shield, to quench all [the] flaming arrows of the evil one. And take the helmet of salvation and the sword of the Spirit, which is the word of God." (Eph 6:16-17)

I want to use that sword in overcoming dangers. I feel a great need for inspiration in understanding the word of the Spirit. We hear comments from time to time deriding the Church's repetitious reading of the same gospels and epistles year after year. "Read that - been there" they scoff. What short sightedness! Every time I hear a familiar text at worship, I wait anxiously for a cleric to help me understand its relevance for me, admitting that I must make an effort also to probe the meaning. I am sometimes disappointed; other times very grateful for some aspect of the reading that I never thought of before. It is the Holy Spirit who inspires the cleric and it is he who inspires me in my private reading. I am not looking for "private interpretation of the scriptures". What I pray for is that the Spirit will help me notice something I previously overlooked.

It's a lot like looking at a painting by one of the masters. You know you have studied it before, perhaps on display at one of the museums. But when you look at it this time, you notice something that your eye missed in the past. The ability of the artist to continue to earn your admiration of his work every time you see something different is part of what makes him or her a master painter.

So with the masterful work of the Holy Spirit in sacred scripture. Each time we pray again over a familiar passage, we may notice something new. For example, in the account of the passion of Our Lord in the gospels, we remember that Peter wept when he heard the cock crow after his denial of Jesus three times. But if we read it carefully in St Luke, we will notice that it was a glance from Our Lord after the cock crowed that made Peter remember what Jesus had said and caused him to go out and weep bitterly.

Again, we all remember that Pilate washed his hands as though to cleanse himself of any part in the crucifixion of Jesus. But if we read carefully in St Matthew, we will notice that Pilate's wife had nagged the governor not to have anything to do with the death of Jesus. (cf. Mt 27:19) We might ask: was Pilate's washing of his hands more to save face with his wife than anything else?

Then there is the purple garment the soldiers of Herod put on Jesus as they mocked him. Many of us have a vivid memory of holy cards showing Jesus in that purple robe as Pilate says "Behold the man". But a careful reading of St Matthew's account shows that the soldiers put on him a scarlet military cloak when they crowned him with thorns, (cf. Mt 27:28) but then stripped him of the cloak and dressed him in his own clothes before leading him away. (cf. Mt 27:31)

We also recall that Simon of Cyrene was pressed into service to carry the cross of Jesus. But we do not have a clear picture of how that was done until we read carefully in St Luke (23:26) that Simon was made to carry it <u>behind</u> Jesus.

With regard to the Holy Spirit, as often as you heard Jesus promise to send the Spirit to the apostles, did you ever notice that he promises to send <u>another</u> paraclete? As we know, the word paraclete etymologically means advocate or one called together. This makes me more aware of the function of the Spirit to be a friend, companion, comforter as well as a giver of strength. Jesus was such a friend; now he will send another friend! Is that a new idea for you? We do not need novelties in our worship to replace sacred readings. The bible is more than enough!

But we must not rely on our own ability to correctly understand the bible. We must seek heavenly inspiration to comprehend its meaning. Where to go for that inspiration? "The Advocate, the holy Spirit, that the Father will send in my name — he will teach you everything and remind you of all that I told you." (Jn 14:26) When Jesus returned to the Father, he did not wish to abandon his followers. He was going to ask the Father to send the very author of scripture to guide mankind's understanding and remembrance of what his teaching involved. "To bring about an ever deeper understanding of revelation, the same Holy Spirit constantly brings faith to completion by his gifts."

(Vatican II, *Dogmatic Constitution on Divine Revelation*, #6) Notice that we are talking about our faith. It is through the gift of the Holy Spirit that man comes by faith to the contemplation and appreciation of the divine plan. (cf. Sir 17:7-8) And "Since their faith is supernatural, God must and does act on men interiorly, to enable them to realize it. Without the effective interior help, which we call grace, we could do nothing profitable for salvation." (Vatican II, *Dogmatic Constitution on Divine Revelation*, footnote 9 of The American Press translation, 1966)

God even wanted people to have confidence in what the Spirit would say about scripture and its lessons, so he established the papacy to protect the people from straying from the true faith that Jesus himself had established. Peter and his successors on the chair of St Peter would have infallibility when they spoke "ex cathedra" about matters of faith and morals.

In one of Augustine's sermons he said "If you believe what you like in the gospels, and reject what you don't like, it is not the gospel you believe, but yourself." Far better that we be guided by the infallibility of the Pope and the teaching of the magisterium so that we accept the whole enchilada.

Some people would have you believe that this power of the Church to explain the teaching of Jesus sometimes goes too far and adds things that Jesus never taught. They would do well to recall how smart and considerate Jesus was in how much teaching he could expect his poor followers to be able to handle. During his farewell speech Jesus said "I have much more to tell you, but you cannot bear it now. But when he comes, the Spirit of truth, he will guide you to all truth." (Jn 16:12)

That guidance continues to this day. Articles of faith, devotional practices — all go through development over time. The mysteries of our faith are exactly that: mysteries. It should be no wonder that they are revealed through the Church over time. Only after much prayerful investigation as to the meaning of sacred scripture, the beliefs of the people of God through the centuries, the teaching of ecclesial luminaries, and the revelations of Jesus, his Blessed Mother and the saints does the Church find it appropriate to speak with certainty about what God wants us to believe and to honor. Such is the development of right order in our day, the domain of the Holy Spirit. "This tradition which comes from the apostles develops in the Church with the help of the Holy Spirit. This happens through the contemplation and study made by believers, who treasure these things in their hearts. [cf. Lk 2:19, 51] " (Vatican Council II, *Dogmatic Constitution on Divine Revelation*, #8)

"The teaching office of the Church reaches only what has been handed on, listening to it carefully, guarding it scrupulously and explaining it faithfully with the help of the Holy Spirit and presents it for belief as divinely revealed." (Vatican II, *Dogmatic Constitution on Divine Revelation*, #10)

The two references to Luke's gospel mentioned above by the Council fathers suggests that our Blessed Mother can be a model in ferreting out the full truth. "Mary kept all these things, reflecting on them in her heart" (Lk 2:19) And "He went down with them and came to Nazareth, and was obedient to them; and His mother kept all these things in her heart." (Lk 2:51) There was a very practical reason for the evangelist to record not once, but twice, that Mary reflected on these happenings and kept them in her heart.

As Pope St John Paul 11 said, Mary was the memory for the early Church. After Jesus returned to the Father, I was she who could remind the new believers of what Jesus did and said. After all, she was his most constant companion. She mothered him for thirty years in their private life, and faithfully followed him around for three years in his public life, including his passion and death. She was a warehouse of information about the Messiah, and as she reflected on the past she was inspired by her spouse, the Spirit, to fully understand its meaning. We assume it was

I Believe in the Holy Spirit?

she who passed on to the evangelists a lot of the details about the early life of Jesus because she was the only one around then.

When we reflect on what we read/hear in the scriptures, we should imitate Mary. She kept going over these things for all those years in her mind. She never got tired of remembering, especially the happy times, as all mothers do. It is said that in order to have faith, one must have a memory of past experiences, events and the people that have formed that faith. Memories are also needed for hope, because it is the recollection of periods of light and bliss that will sustain us in times of darkness, which come to us all.

Other translations of the above two quotations from Saint Luke use the word "ponder" instead of "reflect". Synonyms are: deliberate, ruminate, think deeply about something. Ponder suggests painstaking care about something weighty, usually in terms of its outcome or significance. Some go so far as to say it means to look at something from every angle, to almost argue with oneself so as to grasp it totally. This is a far cry from the ease with which some people glibly throw around the words of the bible as if their meaning should be obvious to anyone.

Arguing with myself can be productive if I stay at it, but meditating on them with others may be more fruitful. In my experience, sharing the thoughts of this new mind can be very enlightening and appreciated. Bible study groups should do more than listen to academic explanations of the holy book. People really want to glean what they can from the bible, which is why it is still the most popular book ever printed. What pays off is people gathering together in reasonably sized groups to read the sacred scripture and then share what the passages mean to them in their faith filled life. When someone shares how meaningful the word of God has been in his/her life, no one goes to sleep!

A common opportunity to experience such personal applications of the bible to one's personal life is a retreat.

Most retreats rely heavily on the words of the Holy Spirit in the bible. Did you ever make a retreat? As the word suggests, this is when you go apart from your daily activities (usually to a place set up for quiet meditation) and devote 1 or 3 or 7 or more days to prayer and private conversation with the Lord. This is an opportunity for the new mind given you by the Holy Spirit to focus on important things like improving the spiritual life of yourself, your family and your community. Every one of our hearts needs renewal from time to time and a retreat is a sure way to get the medicine given by Jesus to have our hearts renewed time and time again.

Anyone who made a Cursillo retreat will have experienced just that: the inspiring effect of someone like yourself sharing what his/her faith has come to mean. The Cursillo movement is a Catholic-based training program that started in Majorca, Spain, in the year 1944. A group of men put together a week-long training event for Catholics preparing to make a pilgrimage to the Shrine of St. James at Compostela. Later, the training was shortened to three days and adapted to target change in community life rather than prepare for pilgrimage. The full title of the event is *Cursillos de Christiandad*, which means "little courses in Christianity" or "short course of Christianity." Cursillo retreats are offered in most American dioceses each year.

In such retreats Cursillistas listen to fifteen different spiritual talks about the Christian life. Leaders of Cursillo emphasize the non-academic nature of the course: the talks relate real-life experiences, which become the basis for small-group discussions. Along with the testimonies are times of music, prayer, Christian service, and contemplation. The Eucharist is a big part of such a retreat. All talks are rooted in the bible. And the Holy Spirit is seen to be the driving force behind all discussions.

He inspires prophets

Mention of prophecies reminds us to look for further documentation and explanation of inspiration in the Old Testament and all that the prophets wrote about therein. Much of the empowering we read about in the Old Testament was to inspire human representatives of God. In the case of prophets, they became God's messengers, representing him in delivering the message. This is evident from the many times when a prophet simply passed on a single message from God.

Sometimes that message was not well received, as for example in 2 Chron. 24:20 when the prophet Zechariah was stoned to death because the message was a rebuke to his king. The latter may or may not have appreciated the source of the message. But he was the first recorded example of "killing the messenger" when the news was not flattering or otherwise pleasing.

More frequently, prophets were a special kind of Jewish leader empowered by God to provide advice to the people, based on inspiration they received from the Lord in relation to situations confronting the chosen people. They were also delivering messages from God, as can be seen from the numerous times when their speech began with the words: "Thus says the Lord: ..."

The message could be a warning, a prediction, a command or whatever. The point always was that these humans were giving voice to words not of their own choice, but that of God. As Isaiah described his function:

> "The spirit of the Lord GOD is upon me,
> because the Lord has anointed me;
> He has sent me to bring glad tidings to the lowly,
> to heal the brokenhearted,
> To proclaim liberty to the captives
> and release to the prisoners.
> To announce a year of favor from the Lord

and a day of vindication by our God;
to comfort all who mourn; ... (Is 61:1-2).

The prophet was here referring to the restoration of Zion. Jesus later cited this passage as a description of his own mission in the New Testament. In both cases it is the only Spirit's words that are being spoken.

Isaiah is most cited with regard to his prophecies about the coming Messiah. He described Jesus as born of a virgin, as a servant leader, as suffering for our sins. He also gave a list of gifts that would belong to Jesus, which we now cite as specific gifts given to anyone who receives the Holy Spirit:

"The spirit of the Lord shall rest upon him:
a spirit of wisdom and of understanding,
A spirit of counsel and of strength,
a spirit of knowledge and of fear of the Lord, ..."
(Is 11:1-2)

A brief list of prophets who played a significant role in guiding the continual development of the Israelites under the inspiration of the Holy Spirit would include Elijah, Elisha, Ezekiel, Isaiah, Jeremiah, Jonah, and Malachi.

How do we know they were acting under the guidance of the Holy Spirit? Recall, for example, the words of Elisha when he recognized he was to carry on the work of his master, Elijah, who offered him to ask for anything he wanted: "May I receive a double portion of your spirit." (2 Kings 2:9)

Ezekiel explains his authority as a spokesperson for the Lord this way: "As he spoke to me, spirit entered into me and set me on my feet, and I heard the one who was speaking say to me: 'Son of man, I am sending you to the Israelites... But you shall say to them: Thus says the Lord God!'..." (Ez. 2:2,4)

Nehemiah regrets the people not following the messages from the prophets when he wrote: "You were patient with them for many years, bearing witness against them through your spirit, by means of your prophets..." (Neh. 9:30)

All of these tend to confirm that the people in general recognized that the well-known prophets had been inspired by the Spirit to fulfill their mission. It was not their advice or prediction or remonstrance; it was the Lord's being made known to the people by individuals known to be in touch with or "filled by" the Spirit, as for example, the prophet Micah:

> "But as for me, I am filled with power,
> with the spirit of the Lord,
> with authority and with might..." (Mic. 3:8)

That these prophecies came directly from the Holy Spirit is made perfectly clear by the words of Saint Peter: "Know this first of all, that there is no prophecy of scripture that is a matter of personal interpretation, for no prophecy ever came through human will; but rather human beings moved by the holy Spirit spoke under the influence of God" (2 Pet. 1:20-21)

Prophets underwent a two-fold experience with the Holy Spirit. They first received the message from God and then had to deliver it. The first step is called "revelation"; the second, "proclamation." The Spirit was involved in both steps.

"Revelation" occurred in a number of different ways, At times it was just a matter of finding the word of God revealed in holy writ, in the law, or in what had been spoken or written by previous prophets. The work of the Holy Spirit there was enlightening the messenger so that his knowledge was greater and truer than it had been.

At other times the Spirit was more active in telling the messenger what to say or write and when, how and where to say or write it. In those instances also the mind was in possession of more knowledge than it had before. Here it was the Holy Spirit who was the prime mover, initiating what would become a transmission of information. The messengers did not even know they would be involved in this message until the Spirit did something. It might be a vision; it might be a dream; it might just be a voice.

The simplest example of this kind of revelation taking place might be the episode in 1 Sam 3:4-14. You will recall young Samuel was asleep and heard his name being called. Not once, not twice, but three times he heard what he thought was the call of his teacher, Eli, only to find out that he was being called by God to receive a message, which he finally did accept on the fourth call from God.

The work of the Spirit with regard to the "proclamation" part of the prophecies involved the imparting of the power to address superiors, to speak in foreign languages, to travel great distances, to overcome a variety of obstacles, etc. All this might be called empowerment to be able to complete a task.

A good number of the prophets were called upon to deliver messages to the king of a recalcitrant population, which meant those prophets were also empowered with strength that might literally be called "super human" to overcome the natural fear of being contradicted or outright condemned by selfish interests/enemies of the Lord. Jesus himself was to say later: "A prophet is not without honor except in his native place and in his own house." (Mt 13:57)

We are not all going to be prophets. But all Christians are called to courageously live the Gospels in our homes, neighborhoods, parish communities and wherever the Spirit leads us, and give witness to Jesus. Today is an era of political correctness. That causes more Christians to cautiously couch their words of evangelization in a way not "to insult" non-believers. "For God did not give us a spirit of cowardice, but rather of power and love and self-control." (2 Tim 1:7) What do you say to people who support the movement to guarantee an income to people who choose not to work? What do you say when the news turns to a vote to legalize sex "businesses" like prostitution? We must not sugar coat the teaching of Jesus. After all, he did not, which is why he wound up on a Cross!

He inspires in the New Testament

Inspiration did not end with the close of the Old Testament. Consider first how the Spirit came with Jesus to Mary. "The holy Spirit will come upon you, and the power of the Most High will overshadow you..." (Lk 1:35) Having no mortal father, he was the son of Mary and the Son of God by the overshadowing of the Hoy Spirit. Taking then "the genes" of the Spirit, so to speak, Our Lord was completely filled with the Holy Spirit. His divine nature was attached to the Father by the Spirit, and his human nature was infused by that same Spirit.

Then "After...Jesus also had been baptized and was praying, heaven was opened and the holy Spirit descended upon him in bodily form like a dove..." (Lk 3:21-2) The is frequently referred to as Jesus being baptized by the Holy Spirit. Because Jesus was already filled with the spirit, the descent of the dove, and the words of the Father which followed, "You are my beloved Son; with you I am well pleased" (Lk 3:22), were more of a message to all the beholders than any kind of increase of the spirit. We might also learn from this additional infusion that the Spirit needs to keep coming to us. It is not a brief or one time indwelling.

This is borne out by the words of Luke, after Jesus has been tempted by the devil in the desert. "Jesus returned to Galilee in the power of the Spirit... He taught in their synagogues and was praised by all." (Lk 4:14-15) Again, when he spoke in his home town of Nazareth, Jesus said that the prophecy of Isaiah (Is 61:1-2) "The Spirit of the Lord is upon me, because he has anointed me..." referred to him (Lk 4:21). Further, Jesus insisted that the good that he did, for example driving out demons, was by the Spirit of God. (cf. Mt 12:28)

The entire ministry of Jesus was performed with the power of the Holy Spirit. This was first foretold in the Book of Isaiah, sometimes called the "the fifth Gospel" or "the Gospel of the Old Testament", so much of Isaiah's prophecies having to do with the Messiah and his mission. When he speaks of the coming of the mysterious person (later to be identified as Jesus) Isaiah connects this person and his mission to the action of the Spirit of God, aka the Spirit of the Lord.

> "But a shoot shall sprout from the stump of Jesse,
> and from his roots a bud shall blossom.
> The spirit of the Lord shall rest upon him:
> a spirit of wisdom and understanding.
> A spirit of counsel and of strength,
> a spirit of knowledge and of fear of the Lord,
> and his delight shall be the fear of the Lord."
> (Is 11:1)

And again, "Now the Lord God has sent me, and his spirit." (Is 48:16) The apostles recognized that Jesus was being spoken of here as being sent by the Spirit, as St Peter gave witness in the house of the centurion Cornelius: "how God anointed Jesus of Nazareth with the holy Spirit and power. He went about doing good and healing all those oppressed by the devil, for God was with him." (Acts 10:38)

Such couldn't be so were it not for the constant praying that Jesus did, often going off by himself to converse with the Father, especially before major events in his life. He was impelled to the work of his ministry when the same Holy Spirit descended upon him in prayer. He spoke of remaining in the Father and the Father in him, which is, of course, the Hoy Spirit as we now understand the mystery of the Trinity. The final mention of this occurs after the Resurrection when St Paul says: "`If the Spirit of the one who raised Jesus from the dead..." (Rom 8:11). Jesus is never separated from the Holy Spirit and is constantly renewed by that Spirit, as an example for us all.

"Christ's whole work is in fact a joint mission of the Son and the holy Spirit." (CCC 727) Countless times Jesus alludes to the Holy Spirit, so close are they in teaching the true faith. Thus he tells Nicodemus that being reborn means being born from above by the Spirit. (Jn 3:5-8) And when talking about water to the Samaritan woman, He says: "God is Spirit, and those who worship him must worship in Spirit and truth." (Jn 4:24) So too with regard to Jesus as the source of living water: "Let anyone who thirsts come to me and drink. Whoever believes in me, as scripture says:

> "...'Rivers of living water will flow from within him' " (Jn 7:37-38)

The evangelist explains "He said this in reference to the Spirit that those who came to believe in him were to receive." (Jn 7:39) Likewise, when teaching about God's answer to our prayers, Jesus said "If you then, who are wicked, know how to give good gifts to your children, how much more will the Father in heaven give the holy Spirit to those who ask him?" (Lk 11:13)

After the Resurrection and ascension of Jesus, we see the inspiration of the Holy Spirit coming to the aid of all those entrusted with carrying on the work of Jesus. Its first manifestation occurred at Pentecost. The band of early followers of Jesus were holed up in the upper room for days after the Ascension, awaiting the promised Spirit who would make all things known to them and who would give them the audacity to speak out publicly proclaiming their belief in the risen Christ.

"When the time for Pentecost was fulfilled,, they were all in one place together. And suddenly there came from the sky a noise like a strong driving wind, and it filled the entire house in which they were. Then there appeared to them tongues as of fire, which parted and came to rest on each of them. And they were all filled with the holy Spirit and began to speak in different tongues, as the Spirit enabled them to proclaim" (Acts 2: 1-4).

This familiar passage says it all. These disciples were to be permanent messengers of God, missioned to spread the Good News, the story of Jesus Christ and his saving life, death and resurrection. To help their simple minds to realize something wonderful was taking place, the Spirit came like a driving wind and appeared as fiery tongues and powered them to speak in all kinds of foreign languages: all physical signs that what they had to say to the onlookers and then to the ends of the earth was indeed the result of their being "filled with the Spirit", a phrase known to men in all ages to mean they were passing on something from God.

But the Holy Spirit was not done then either. Peter was informed by the Spirit when he and other early disciples were brought before the Jewish Sanhedrin. "Then Peter, filled with the holy Spirit, answered them..." (Acts 4:8) After Peter and the others were released and went back to the Christian community, "...the place where they were gathered shook, and they were all filled with the holy Spirit and continued to speak the word of God with boldness." (Acts 4:31) When Paul and Barnabas began their first mission, "sent forth by the holy Spirit" (Acts 13:4), they were opposed first by Elymas, the magician. "But Saul, also known as Paul, filled with the holy Spirit, looked intently at him and said, 'You son of the devil, you enemy of all that is right'..." (Acts 13:9-10)

This kind of work on the part of the Spirit did not cease with the prophets of the Old Testament or with the early followers of

Christ recorded in the Acts and other early Christian documents. We continue to need the inspiration of the Holy Spirit.

Moses had wished in his time that prophets would arise to keep God's chosen people on the straight and narrow path. At the time of Joel, God spoke through this prophet and said

> "Then afterward I will pour out
> my spirit upon all mankind.
> Your sons and daughters shall prophesy,
> your old men shall dream dreams,
> your young men shall see visions;…" (Joel, 3:1)

Revelation of heaven sent information will always be an important work of the Spirit. Once again this attribute of the third Person of the Trinity is to bring to completion a work of God toward humans: planned by the Father, effected by the Son, brought to a successful end by the Holy Spirit.

This was true in the early Christian church. "When they had brought them in and made them stand before the Sanhedrin, the high priest questioned them, 'We gave you strict orders [did we not?] to stop teaching in that name. Yet you have filled Jerusalem with your teaching and want to bring this man's blood upon us. But Peter and the apostles said in reply 'We must obey God rather than men. The God of our ancestors raised Jesus, though you had him killed by hanging him on a tree. God exalted him at his right hand as leader and savior to grant Israel repentance and forgiveness of sins. We are witnesses of these things, as is the holy Spirit that God has given to those who obey him.' " (Acts 5: 27-32)

Now we give the same witness with the help of the Holy Spirit by what is called evangelization, defined as preaching the Gospel, converting to Christianity, or to give witness to Christ. We ourselves are not able to understand who Jesus is on our own strength, intellect or power. First, then, the Holy Spirit aids us in moving from our limited intellectual perception of who Christ is and what he has done for us to such a deep relationship with Jesus that we must tell others about him. "When the Advocate comes whom I will send you from the Father, the Spirit of truth that proceeds from the Father, he will testify to me." (Jn 15:26) The Holy Spirit then inspires us to give witness to Christ by our words and actions.

St Paul mentions two steps in order to appear with Jesus in eternal glory. If we believe in Christ we are saved; if we profess him on our lips, we will be with him in glory. So it is not just what we think in our heart; we must also give witness to him by our speech, which as we have seen is the result of being inspired by the Holy Spirit. "Evangelization is never possible without the Holy Spirit. It must be said that the Holy Spirit is the evangelizer." (Pope Paul VI, *Evangelii Nuntiandi*, #75)

He gives gifts and fruits

"The Most Holy Trinity gives the baptized sanctifying grace, the grace of *justification* ... giving them the power to live and act under the prompting of the Holy Spirit through the gifts of the Holy Spirit." (CCC, 1266)

The gifts referred to are those mentioned by Isaiah (Is 11: 2) and enumerated in #1832 of the Catechism; namely wisdom, understanding, counsel, fortitude, knowledge, piety and fear of the Lord. We are told there that these gifts are permanent dispositions which make us docile in following the promptings of the Holy Spirit. (CCC, 1830) We have them then from the time of our baptism as the means of being able to keep our vows to live a holy life.

If Augustine is praying for such inspiration, it is not because he does not have these gifts, but because he wants them to be ameliorated. He wants them to bear the fruits of the Holy Spirit, which are the "perfections that the Holy Spirit forms in us as the first fruits of eternal glory." (CCC, 1832) Isaiah mentioned them in the Old Testament (cf Is 11:2-3) and the tradition of the church lists 12 of them beginning with those mentioned by St. Paul (Gal 5:22-23); namely, charity (love), joy, peace, patience, kindness, goodness, generosity, gentleness, faithfulness, modesty, self-control, and chastity.

Love is always mentioned first, because the Holy Spirit is love itself. "God is love" (1Jn 4:8, 16) and love is his first fruit, containing all others. "...the love of God has been poured out into our hearts through the holy Spirit that has been given to us." (Rom 5:5)

Closely related to the gifts are other benefits given by the Holy Spirit and more properly called "charisms" (discussed in the chapter on empowerment).

The typical Christian is in need of inspiration, not so much in order to pass on a special message from God, but in order to teach, to clarify the words of scripture or teaching of the Church. This could be in the ministry of education or the raising of children in the faith.

But all Christians need the indwelling of the Spirit in order to hear and understand the message of the divine Sower. What a clear picture was spoken by Jesus when he taught his followers through the parable of the sower. While each of us want to be fertile ground for the message of Jesus, we all recognize that we all too often are not quite that pure of heart.

At times we are hard of heart, like the path Jesus mentions. Pope Francis says the seed then bounces off this impermeable heart as if off a "street", so it does not enter. At other times, we are more open to hearing the word, but we are like rocky ground, meaning we welcome the Lord, wishing to love, to pray, to bear witness; but we tire easily and do not persevere because our heart has no depth and the rocks of laziness prevail.

A final situation mentioned in the parable concerns the state of our heart which can be compared to thorny ground. Here we might conjure up the image of the lamb caught in the briar patch. Such is the state of our soul when we allow the cares of the world, the pursuit of riches, the selfish indulgence in pleasure, and all the other manifestations of self-centeredness to block the reception of the word.

The work of an inspiring Holy Spirit is to melt the hardness of our heart, to water and cultivate the deep roots of faith, and to tear out the thorny vices that inhabit our heart. This is the prayer of Augustine so that his words may be holy or beneficial when spoken to others, as they will emanate from a heart that has been made fertile by the indwelling of the Holy Spirit.

And what is the result of this further overflowing of the Holy Spirit? He gives gifts for powers beyond human natural powers; he imparts boldness in carrying out our mission or service to God and his people; he fills our mind with apprehension of the truth, especially regarding Christ — in a word, he takes possession of our faculties.

This can be seen in the Pentecost event; for the very first action of the apostles was an outpouring of the message of Christ in various languages.

These are indeed very special gifts. But the Spirit gives us countless other gifts, so numerous that we take them for granted. Venerable Fulton J Sheen lists things like friendships, the joys of marriage, the thrill of possession, the sunset and the evening star, masterpieces of art and music, the gold and silver of earth, the industries and comforts of life — all these, he says are gifts that God drops on the roadway of our life. He is hoping that our mind will rise from these beautiful things to him, Beauty itself. (cf. *Remade for Happiness*, copyright 2004, Ignatius Press)

The trouble is that we forget to say thank you. Some say our new Millennials seem to have forgotten the words "Thank You". Maybe so, but we are all guilty of that. My beloved wife, in raising our children, made saying Thank You one of the most important lessons of growing up.

He teaches us how to pray

"The Spirit too comes to the aid of our weakness; for we do not know how to pray as we ought, but the Spirit itself intercedes with inexpressible groanings." (Rom 8:26) We are told to ask, to seek, to knock unceasingly. At the conclusion of every Collect prayer at Mass, we ask "through Our Lord, Jesus Christ, your Son, who lives and reigns with you in the unity of the Holy Spirit, one God forever and ever. Amen." This not only expresses our belief in the Trinity; it also suggests that our prayers are to be offered in union with the Spirit who will see that they reach the ears of the Father.

When Jesus told his disciples not to worry what to say (Mt 10:19) because it will be given to them what to say by the inspiration of the Spirit, he was not referring only to when they would be handed over to evil men. He was encouraging peace of mind and heart as was always his wont. He was telling us how to pray. Be at peace, do your asking, but then leave it in the hands of God as to how to answer your praying. The best example of this is how our Blessed Mother asked something of her beloved Son. When her friends at their wedding feast ran short of wine, she said simply "They have no wine". (Jn 2:3) She did not tell Jesus what to do about it. She did not presume to tell him how to answer her gentle request. She as much as said "Take care of it, please." The Spirit teaches us to make our needs known — even though God knows what they are before we tell him — and then leave it up to him.

The peace that can be found in prayer deserves mention at this point. All too often when we pray it is because we are in great need. Things have been building up: illness, broken relationships, financial setbacks, and the like. And by the time we realize we should put these problems in the hands of God, we are quite worked up over them. And our prayers take on the aura of impatience and frustration that we are feeling. Whoa, we should slow down, try to be at peace and speak to our Father quietly, not screaming in despair.

Praying as the Our Father teaches might be the best way to do this. As Jesus taught us how to pray, we talk to God about himself first, give him praise and thanksgiving, and only then make known what we seek. This measured approach to our conversation with God will in itself have a calming effect and bring peace in our heart. Reading the lives of the saints will quickly reveal how peaceful their lives became when they learned to commune with the almighty in this way. They found themselves forgetting about themselves and spending more time literally raising their minds and hearts to God. Their thoughts became blissful imaginings of what true happiness consists of. I think of Saint Martin de Porres, the humble mulatto lay Dominican brother of Lima, Peru at the end of the 17th century, whose constant advice to be at peace with oneself led him to long periods of silent prayer before the crucifix and mystical levitation. He was literally caught up in his prayer and had no concerns about his life because he turned to Christ.

A sign of our times: more people are turning to crack than to Christ. They say they are looking for an escape from their miserable lives. People are voting to legalize recreational drugs. They are legalizing psychedelic mushrooms. They want to lose contact with reality and float in a sea of beautiful images. What they really should do is read the lives of our mystical saints who found the only worthwhile way to absent themselves from the material world is to be caught up in the wonders of spirituality. Communing with God will be seen as such a great "high" that they will never think of drugs again, and the after effects will not be hangovers.

Conclusion

It would seem that a second very important role of the Holy Spirit is to inspire us, to fill our minds with holy thoughts, to fill us with gifts and fruits, to give us the courage to stand up and be counted as one worthy to be called a follower of Christ. No matter what my calling in this life might be, the Spirit is anxious to make of me a missionary of the word, a purveyor of the Good News, a beacon of light to those around me in all humility speaking his mind.

A BRIEF CONVERSATION WITH THE HOLY SPIRIT

Come, O Holy Spirit and walk with me as my constant companion.

Dear Spirit of light, anxious to send the warmth of your light into my heart, I beseech you: take up your rest in my heart! Fill the heart which you have made. Flood my dull senses with the light of your love. I see now that a request for inspiration means simply for your Spirit to be in me. I can then be strong in practicing my faith and, by giving witness to all you mean to me, to be able to pass on some of the Word to others.

My puny intellect is incapable of grasping the complete meaning of the messages you send me by way of scripture, and tradition, and the teaching of the church, and the preaching of your clerics, and the whispering of my guardian angel. So I ask you to inspire me with sufficient grasp of what you are calling me to do that I will not disappoint you.

"O Come, Holy Spirit, Creator blest, and in my heart take up thy rest" is a hymn we sing to you often, especially during your holy season of Pentecost. May I pay more attention to this prayer about your sevenfold gifts, or characteristics of yourself.

I would like to thank you for teaching me how to appreciate the Old Testament in recent years. Members of other religious denominations have often embarrassed me with their ability to cite the words of our ancestors. To my chagrin they often put me to shame with their memory of the exact words. They have memorized many verses, suggesting they have studied them and read them over and over. As you know, I have been able to put aside time for private reading of sacred scripture, but aside from a few psalms I used to spend time mostly from the Gospels, without adequate appreciation of the books of the Old Testament.

    I am so much in need of a new mind. I am getting on in years, but it is not too late. Help me, Holy Spirit, to not only know what you have written in the holy bible, but to understand what is there underneath the mere words. Please keep making scripture a joy to read, to hear, to have opened for me. When the daily readings seem to be repetitious, give me new insight into their meanings. Help me to not only listen, but to meditate, to ponder what they mean for my daily life. Thank you for the years of faith sharing meetings with bible study groups. Thank you for the give and take those sessions provided. Thank you for the inspirations you gave to my fellow students of your holy word and their courage in speaking their new minds also.

    To you, O Spirit, I lift up my soul for you to reshape so I may avoid all that is unholy. I trust you; let me not be disappointed. Form in me a new mind with a realistic view of materialism, to which I might become enslaved in my hunger for consumption and false pleasures.

    I place in your hands my heart, my soul, the deep recesses of my being wherein dwell those beliefs and thoughts that govern my actions so you may guide me in the way of the Gospel.

    In that regard, I have only recently begun to probe the way you inspired your many messengers (prophets) in order to make known what you expected from your chosen people. While Moses and Isaiah and what they had to say about deliverance and the Suffering Servant have been often enough in my mind, asking me about Elias and David and Job and so many others would have shown a deep vacuum. Please broaden my vistas so that I can become more familiar with what their words can mean to me. "changing the things that need changing".

Help me to be faithful to my promise to spend at least ten minutes each day in slow and thoughtful reading of your words in the bible.

Come, wise Counsellor, inspire in me thoughts of wisdom for those seeking advice, words of comfort for those who are afflicted, and actions of succor for those in need.

Thank you for reminding me that holy means to be on fire and to be separate. Just as pondering means a lot more energetic meditating, so my aspiration for my words to be holy must include expecting them to show me on fire with love for your word and to be set apart or different from the lukewarm.

With St. Augustine, I pray: MOVE IN ME, O HOLY SPIRIT, THAT MY WORDS TOO MAY BE HOLY.

THE HOLY SPIRIT AS LOVER

Attract my heart, O Holy Spirit,
that I may love only what is holy.

Here Saint Augustine wants to be so in love with the Spirit as to find nothing attractive that is not holy. Augustine here wants his heart to find the Spirit attractive. He recognizes that the pure of heart will be attached to holiness. He wants his heart to find gratification in the Spirit, which means he will love the third Person of the Blessed Trinity. He is asking the Spirit to show Himself so strongly that his heart will be drawn to Him and find no satisfaction elsewhere. In terms of the work of the Holy Spirit, we believe that:

He unites through love
He consoles, comforts
He draws us only to what is holy
He speaks through images

He unites through love

Love is a relationship between two entities. We say "I love ice cream" or "I love football" or "I love Hawaii", or "I love classical music" or "I love my daughter". Why do we say that? Because we found something attractive about that food, that place, that form of entertainment, that person. And like the force of a magnet, we are drawn to it or them. We find some gratification in being with that food or place, etc. We shun things or people which we find unattractive.

It sounds as though Augustine perceives the Spirit as principally attractiveness or love. This is clearly the result of his work on the Trinity. He understood and preached that what held the three Persons together in one God was their relationship. The Father and the Son were linked by their mutual love which was so strong that it was a third Person. In other words, that third Person, the Holy Spirit, was love itself. And since it was this love that kept them all together, love might also be described as union or the power of keeping individuals together.

Pope Benedict XVI, commented on Augustine's struggle to understand the Spirit, in his speech on the World Youth Day vigil, Saturday night at the Randwick Racecourse in Sydney. July 19, 2008. The pope said it was resolved by his view of the Spirit as being what is shared by the Father and the Son.

Augustine's theology of the Holy Spirit developed from understanding that the Holy Spirit is truly divine to an exposition of the Holy Spirit as the love of God who maintains peace and order within creation. Augustine taught that God is a Trinity of love. "God is love." (1Jn 4:16) He argued that while these words refer to the Trinity as a whole, they express a particular characteristic of the Holy Spirit. What is special about him is what is shared by the Father and the Son. The Spirit's particular quality is to be a unifying agent. It is a unity of loved communion: a unity of persons in a relationship of constant giving, the Father and the Son giving themselves to each other. Once we are infused with the Holy Spirit, we respond to the unifying presence, and we give ourselves to one another in the service which Jesus taught as the second of only two commandments.

Follow his logic: God is love; God cannot be love unless there is something for him to love. But if that something were not part of himself, he would not be perfect. Therefore God must be love inside himself. The Father loves; the Son is loved, as was revealed in the baptism of Jesus; and the Holy Spirit is the love that flows between them and binds them together, and who moreover binds believers to God.

Further, reflecting on the lasting nature of this love — "... whoever remains in love remains in God and God in him" (1Jn 4:16) — Augustine wondered whether it is love or the Holy Spirit which grants this. He concluded that the Holy Sport makes us remain in God and God in us; yet it is love that effects this. The Spirit therefore is God as love. God sharing himself with us as gift is the Holy Spirit. After his conversion and reflecting on the many years of turbulence in his restless mind, Augustine wrote that oft-quoted phrase "Thou hast made us for thyself, O Lord, and our heart is restless until it finds its rest in thee." And again "Late have I loved you, beauty so old and so new: late have I loved you." Since the Holy Spirit is God's love personified, it is to that Lord that the bishop spoke.

This ought to be my first understanding of the love of the Holy Spirit, namely that I love God because he first loves me. He loves not as a group, but me individually. He loves me by name. He has engraved my image in his heart. Venerable Fulton J. Sheen used to say that there seems to be one small piece missing out of every human heart. Because when God made your heart he found it so so lovable that he kept a small sample of it in heaven.

What's more, he loves me with his whole heart, because he cannot love as we do, in pieces; he loves with his whole heart, infinitely. The saints understood this and were enthralled by it. Servant of God Dorothy Day wrote that a mystic may be called a person in love with God. Not one who loves God, but who is *in love with God*. (cf. *Dorothy Day Selected Writings*, Robert Ellsberg, ed.) The two are one.

Once we are inflamed with the love of the Spirit, our relationship with each other will be a reflection of that relationship with God. And if we live by the Spirit, walking in the Spirit, we will be bearing the fruit of the Spirit, called thus in

Galatians 5:22,23, because its source is the Spirit. It begins with love and is summed up in love.

In 1 Cor 14, Paul called on the Corinthians to pursue love (verse 1) and to strive for love. He talks at length once more about how they should minister to one another. He points out that love is the guiding principle in using their gifts of ministry.

We also acknowledge the role of the Holy Spirit in uniting us in the mystical body of Christ during Mass. We pray for this unity in the Second Eucharistic Prayer: "Humbly we pray that, partaking of the Body and Blood of Christ, we may be gathered into one by the Holy Spirit." We are one in the Lord, but it is the power of the Spirit that makes it so. And more times than not we conclude the Collect of the Mass with the words: "Through Our Lord Jesus Christ, your Son, who lives and reigns with you in the unity of the Holy Spirit, one God, for ever and ever." Just as the Spirit is the force for unity in the Trinity itself, his love is what unites us as his believers. "He (the Holy Spirit) begets to a new life those who believe in Christ. He gathers them into one People of God, which is a chosen race, a royal priesthood, a holy nation, a purchased people." (Vatican Council II, *Decree on the Missionary Activities of the Church*, #15)

Our hearts should also embrace those not yet in full communion with the Church, for the gift of charity given by the Holy Spirit demands it. The unity of all Christians is desired by many today and is even sought by many who not yet believe in Christ. Non-Catholics are joined to us in the Holy Spirit, for to them he gives his graces and gifts, and is thereby operative among them. (cf. Vatican II, *Dogmatic Constitution on the Church*, #15) Our duty is to pray that all be responsive to the impulses of the Holy Spirit, for our unity can be a harbinger of unity and peace for all the world. (cf. Vatican II, *Pastoral Constitution for the Church in the Modern World*, #92) For this reason we celebrate the Church Unity Octave each January. And during the Professions of Good Friday's liturgy the Church prays for the unity of all different sects, religions, and pagans.

In terms of our search for his role, since he is God himself eternally giving himself, like a never ending spring pouring forth nothing less than himself, if the Spirit is love, can it not be said that love is one of the things the Holy Spirit does? We might say one of the important functions of the Spirit is loving unity. This aspect of the Holy Spirit is referenced frequently in sacred scripture; for example, in Romans 5:5 "The love of God has been poured out into our hearts through the holy Spirit that has been given to us." The gift of the Spirit refers to the baptism in the Holy Spirit. This is how God's love continues to pour out for us, a continuing "work" of the Holy Spirit.

St Paul explains in 1 Corinthians how this "behavior" of the Holy Spirit builds up the spiritual life of the Christian. In this letter, Paul is gently berating inappropriate use of the many gifts of the one Spirit. He reminds them that knowledge, prophecy, tongues, curing and the like are all gifts, and given by the Spirit to whomsoever he wishes. There should be no jealousy in the community about these gifts, for they all come from the same Spirit and are to be used to spread the Gospel. He takes knowledge as an example, and says that it, as developed by human reason, may cause a person to put on airs; it might breed pride, arrogance, conceit. But knowledge, animated by the love of the Spirit, causes that man to know God and promote the good of all. (cf. 1 Cor 8:1)

Paul goes on at some length to insist that the spiritual gifts being enjoyed by the new followers of Christ will not lead to a successful ministry to the brethren without being inspired by love, which is a gift of the Spirit. Speaking in tongues without this love, can be compared to a noisy gong or clanging symbols. (cf.1 Cor 13:1)

What is the result on the part of the faithful if one's heart is drawn to this divine love? Being attracted to Him as the sole object of our human affection, we will love only what is holy. Possessing our soulmate, as the groom his bride, we will not seek gratification elsewhere. Our union with God, the Spirit, will be so strong that only what is holy will we find attractive.

Here it is important to note that this will not be a one time thing. This love will never die. We will not turn to other pleasures as though love of God is just a passing fancy. The spirit does not come in a rush and then run out of steam. Being enamored with the magnetic pull of the Spirit is renewed constantly. Sometimes the faithful speak of being born again through baptism as though it occurs only once. Pentecost came to the Apostles in chapter Two of the Acts of the Apostles, accompanied by strong winds and thundering noise to make certain they knew Jesus was fulfilling his promise. But it did not end there. In chapter Four of the same Acts, we find the Apostles being filled with the Holy Spirit while they were at prayer: "After they prayed, the place where they were meeting was shaken. And they were all filled with the Holy Spirit and spoke the Word of God boldly." The marvelous "work" of the Spirit as love endures.

We call ourselves Christians, that is, followers of Christ or Christ-like people. We try to act as he did. We are told to ask: "What would Jesus do (WWJD)? But how do we get to follow his example? By our own devices? Hardly, for these are often patterned after the example of Adam and Eve and the original sin weaknesses we inherited from them. "Now the works of the flesh are obvious: immorality, impurity, licentiousness, idolatry, sorcery, hatreds, rivalry, jealousy, outbursts of fury, acts of selfishness, dissensions, factions, occasions of envy, drinking bouts, orgies and the like." (Gal 5: 19-21).

Instead, we must "be strengthened with power through his Spirit in the inner man." (Eph 3:16) "In contrast, the fruit of the Spirit is love, joy, peace, patience, kindness, generosity, faithfulness, gentleness, self-control." (Gal 5:22-3) We do this by being baptized by the Holy Spirit and blood. Being freed from the slavery of sin, we can be Christ-like. The Holy Spirit will dwell within us and form us after the image of our Savior. We will be Christian.

As the hymn says, "They will know we are Christians by our love, by our love..." ; that is "the fulfillment of the law." (Rom 13:10) Love is the relationship we must have with our God and our neighbors. This is the love of Christ formed in us by the Holy Spirit. We may with certainty then say that union through love is one of the important "functions" of the Holy Spirit so that "you, rooted and grounded in love, may have strength to comprehend ... and to know the love of Christ..." (Eph 3:17-19)

We often pray "Come, Holy Spirit, and kindle in us the fire of your love." We immediately see an image of burning flames. Love is associated with fire. Fire consumes, and we pray that our hearts will be consumed in ardor for the Spirit. We want him to reduce to ashes all other possible objects of our affection so that we are attached to God alone, to be holy.

The root of the word "holy" in Hebrew means "to be on fire". It is the fire of the Spirit, the gift of love, which permits us to be holy. It also means "to be separate". Apart from what? From what is not holy, to be attached to God alone.

The psalmist understood that the Spirit is the source of holiness when he said

> "Do not drive me from your presence,
> nor take from me your holy spirit." (Ps 51:13)

He consoles, comforts

When Jesus was ready to return to the Father, he made an amazing comment to his followers. He said "... it is better for you that I go." (Jn 16:7) We can just imagine them thinking "How can it be to our advantage to be without you, Master?" Jesus was quick to explain: "For if I do not go, the Advocate will not come to you." (Jn 16:7) So in the mind of Jesus, this coming of the new friend was a pretty big thing! How come?

"And I will ask the Father, and he will give you another Advocate to be with you always." (Jn 14:16) In Greek, the word is Paraclete, which literally means "called to one's side" (ad vocatus) or "advocate". We think right away of a lawyer, someone who is standing by our side when we are in trouble. The Holy Spirit then was someone who would be their companion, someone they could have confidence in and trust, especially in times of darkness. It was God's intention from the beginning to walk with man, which is what he did with Adam. But after the fall, man was alone, until God sent his Son named Emmanuel or "God with us". After the Ascension, it fell to the Holy Spirit to be man's advocate, to be by the side of man.

The first thing to remember is that this promise was preceded by a very important condition: "If you love me, you will keep my commandments." (Jn 14:15) Then the advocate is promised. No freebie here! What we must note here is that these words of Jesus were spoken during his farewell discourse, preparing the apostles gathered in the upper room for his departure, namely for his passion and death on the Cross. "I will not leave you orphans" said Jesus. (Jn 14:18)

Because the Spirit was to be sent by Jesus, we may here be talking about the most important function that the Spirit was to undertake, so let's dig a little deeper into the meaning of these words.

Paraclete is often translated as "consoler". That name was very appropriate for the one who would come to the apostles, given their sorrow, frustration and general upset feelings at the pending loss of their leader, who was about to return to the Father. So when he came at Pentecost, the first chore for the Spirit was to restore confidence and the desire to go on in the minds and hearts of these missionaries, who were going to face the world alone.

Some translate paraclete as "comforter". This conjures up the image of a big warm blanket to use on a cold winter night. Note also the word "another" before "Advocate" in Jn 14:16. So Jesus is promising to send them another friend — another, meaning just as Jesus was a friend "I no longer call you slaves ... I have called you friends." (Jn 15:15) This word advocate appears four times in scripture with reference to the Holy Spirit. (Jn14:16; Jn 14:26; Jn 15:26; Jn 16:7) It also appears in 1Jn 2:1 with reference to Jesus. So there should be no doubt that the Spirit will treat the friends of Jesus just as Jesus would. No wonder he is is often called "the Spirit of Jesus".

The comfort of the Holy Spirit is that you have a real & abiding friend who loves you; a real friend will not abandon you in the midst of difficulty. Like a comforter, a friend will encourage you; a friend will be beside you with strength right when it is needed most. Like a counselor, a friend will take time to listen and hear your deepest woes; a friend will offer you wise advice and provide help with difficult decisions.

Since the Holy Spirit is our <u>other</u> companion, repeating the comfort given by Jesus, our first friend and comforter, the Spirit "walks before us, his hands charged with gifts; he walks by our side with a beautiful countenance; he walks behind us with extended arms. He walks before us to smooth the rough places of our paths; he walks at our side as a faithful companion, to cheer, encourage, console and defend us. He walks behind us, to receive us if we fall. He walks before us, that we may follow and imitate him; he walks beside us, that we may not grow lonely on the road, and he walks after us to be the remedy of our evils. In following him, we cannot wander; in traveling in his company we shall be strong and vigorous; and in keeping us intimately united to him, he takes care to prevent the slightest suspicion that, with such a support, we cannot do and suffer all things."

(From *The Spiritual Man Or the Spiritual Life Reduced to its First Principles*, by Jean artist Saint-Sure, 1878)

Jesus said: "But whoever blasphemes against the holy Spirit will never have forgiveness" (Mk 3:29). This apparently was a bothersome thought for Jesus; all three synoptic gospels quote Jesus on this. "Every sin and blasphemy will be forgiven people, but blasphemy against the Spirit will not be forgiven. ... whoever speaks against the holy Spirit will not be forgiven, either in this age or in the age to come." (Mt 12:31-32) And "Everyone who speaks a word against the Son of Man will be forgiven, but the one who blasphemes against the holy Spirit will not be forgiven." (Lk 12:10)

Saint Thomas Aquinas explains that Jesus is referring to a sin that is unforgivable by its very nature, because it excludes the elements through which forgiveness of sin takes place. The blasphemy Jesus speaks of is not simply offending by words; it consists of a refusal to accept salvation which God offers through the Holy Spirit by the power of the Cross. (cf. St. Thomas Aquinas, *SummaTheologica*, IIa-IIae, ques. 14, ans. 3)

If, then, there are some people who do sin against the Holy Spirit, perhaps I can show some appreciation for the comfort the Spirit gives me by returning the favor and offering him my comfort to make up for those sinners.

As a loving parent cuddles a child who is upset at a scratched kneecap, or as a loving friend hugs someone who has lost a family member to death, so the Holy Spirit made his presence known to the apostles and lifted up their spirits so that they would put their sorrow behind them and be re-energized.

Married people can certainly appreciate the efficacy of mutual comfort: whether it's a word of encouragement or a smile of congratulation, or a wink about a private joke, or a kiss of devotedness. In like manner, we feel at home counting on the Holy Spirit to be a close confidant and comforter.

The fire of God, our lover, warms the heart of those who pray for consolation. It makes one feel that all is well with the world again. It kindles a passion for undertaking work that might have been thought to be impossible. It takes our mind off our own difficulties and problems and sheds light on what is ahead.

Giving comfort was a big piece of the ministry of Jesus. If this is the Spirit of Jesus, perhaps he will give the same kind of comfort, which goes beyond words of friendship. When Jesus cured the woman with a hemorrhage he said "Courage, daughter! Your faith has saved you." (Mt 9:22) When Jesus cured the blind Bartimaeus, his friends said "Take courage; get up, he is calling you." (Mk 10:49) When Isaiah foretold the ministry that Jesus was to fulfill, it included "to comfort all who mourn." (Is 61:2)

Note too that Jesus promised the new friend would be always present, always available when we need a shoulder to cry on. The Book of Sirach describes the kind of friend we can find in the Holy Spirit:

> "A faithful friend is a sturdy shelter;
> he who finds one finds a treasure.
> A faithful friend is beyond price,
> no sum can balance his worth.
> A faithful friend is a life-saving remedy…"
> (Sir 6:14-16)

And this consoler is not just there to wipe away our tears; he is very active; he becomes our helper; and he becomes our source of strength.

He attracts us only to what is holy

We have seen that we love what we are attracted to; hence the power of advertisements of all sorts. They pull us this way and that. Cleverly done, they make us almost taste or feel what they are enticing us toward. They can make the object of their pitch so desirous that we must have it. And without delay, "Call or click NOW!!!" Left to our own devices, such come-ons can leave us captive.

When we join St Augustine in this prayer, however, we plead not to be left to our own abilities to discern what is worth our love. The heart is the source of the emotion called love. So we ask the Holy Spirit to attract our heart to what is holy. But it is the five senses that send messages to the heart. So we are asking to help us curtail the pull those senses have on our heart strings. We ask the Spirit to have such as pull on our heart that we surrender it only to what is holy, or set apart. Set apart from what? From anything that keeps us from being pure of heart and attracted only to the supreme Good.

As with everything we might pray for, this request presupposes that we are doing our part. It assumes we open our eyes and ears only to what comes from God; that we touch and smell and taste only what is undefiled. In this modern age, we are beset with so many false claims to be happy that it will be easy to be attracted to something not worth our love. We need to set up some standards for what we watch, what we read, where we go, whom we choose to go with, and the like. For some things there are ratings of decency. Think movies and television. But be aware of what these ratings mean. Because one is an adult, is it therefore OK to wallow in "adult" or "R' or other subliminally dangerous offerings? That is a way of being attracted to exactly what we should avoid.

Toward the end of his long sermon on the mount, Jesus seems to sum up much of his teaching by saying "So, be perfect, just as your heavenly Father is perfect." (Mt 5:48) What kind of advice or order is that! How can we hope to be perfect humans, much less perfect as God? Whatever our concept of perfection for a human might be, it must pale before the epitome of perfection which is God. Either or both would seem to be beyond imagining for us specks of dust!

Being perfect implies attaining the purpose for which we are created. That is the secret of the creative work of God. He made things for a purpose: HIS purpose. If we become perfect we will achieve the end for which he made us. That much might be understandable. The problem then is being told to be perfect as God is perfect. We <u>become</u> perfect, meaning there is progress over time to that stage. We <u>grow</u> in perfection. But for God, perfection is not something attained, but was so from all eternity. We can never hope for that; so what did Jesus mean?

He used that word one other time; namely, when he gave directions to the young man who approached him asking what good he must do to attain eternal life. After discussing the commandments and his observance of them, Jesus sums it up in his case, "If you wish to be perfect, go, sell what you have and give to [the] poor, and you will have treasure in heaven. Then, come follow me." (Mt 19:21) Living a life of voluntary poverty has long been part of the path to perfection as it has been lived by members of religious congregations with the three views of poverty, chastity and obedience. But we are not all called to that way of life.

Maybe the way St Peter put it might be a little more attainable. "...as he who called you is holy, be holy yourselves in every aspect of your conduct." (1Pet 1:15) I can begin to make sense of this advice/command as I hear the word "conduct". Being holy has to do with how I behave. What I do is more concrete for me than the ideal word "perfect". And I have been given many examples of good behavior versus bad behavior. I can equate good behavior with holiness. I can begin to get some help in becoming holy by considering my prayer to the Spirit to help me to be attracted only to what is holy.

I might even recall my early catechism teaching. Why did God make you? God made me to know him, to love him, to serve him in this world and to be happy with him forever in heaven. God created me for sanctification. One of the major themes of Vatican II was that universal call to holiness as part of refreshing the life of the Church as though it had been lost sight of.

This is more in keeping with the other command in the bible to be holy, namely when God told Moses "Speak to the whole Israelite community and tell them: Be holy, for I, the Lord, your God, am holy." (Lev 19:2) This was a universal call to be holy. And it was followed with examples of conduct (revere your parents, keep the Sabbath, move away from idols, etc.)

A few of the attributes of God himself are offered for our imitation. For example, "Merciful and gracious is the Lord, slow to anger, abounding in kindness..." (Ps 103:8) Which was paraphrased by St Paul telling the Ephesians to be kind and merciful, forgiving others as God had forgiven them. (cf. Eph 4:32) Controlling these emotions is something I can comprehend and recognize as part of what I've been taught all my life. Every once in awhile someone starts a campaign to have us all practice "Random Acts of Kindness". Maybe that ought to be a permanent habit, if I'm going to try to be this kind of holy. I got an e-mail the other day — one of those that goes viral because it is appealing to everyone. It was a video showing an elephant carrying in his curled up trunk a lioness' cub, who had passed out from the heat. The elephant was full of kindness carrying the cub to the nearest pool of water, while the mother was marching alongside the elephant. Just shows how dumb animals can be pretty smart and kind to each other. Too bad the social media rarely spreads a worthwhile image like this, instead of all the violent and immoral messages we see on a daily basis!

What is surprising about this call to holiness is that it seems unfair to many people. It means we cannot have any fun. It means we have to be Goody 2-shoes. It means we have to go around with folded hands all day long. And so on. What a desecration of reality! We are made after the image of God.

He is holiness itself. Why should we not be expected to be like him, then, to be holy? It is not a passive endeavor, but rather a continuous choice to deepen one's relationship with God and to then allow this relationship to guide all of one's actions in the world. Holiness requires a radical change in mindset and attitude. The acceptance of the call to holiness places God as our final goal in every aspect of our lives. Fortified by the gifts of the Holy Spirit, we can then progress/mature in holiness; we can become holy as our Father is holy.

He speaks through images

One way the Holy Spirit talks to us is through the various symbols or images we see in his work for us. They are often mentioned when we see him at work without any explanation, trusting that they are self evident. Evident or not, we might get a clearer appreciation for all he does for us if we take the time reflect on what these images or tools of his trade are and what they mean for us.

WATER is very often associated with his work, as in baptism. We should have no problem in seeing the connection of water with cleansing of the soul, because the first property of water is to make something clean, whether it is the water we use in our washing machines to cleanse our clothes, or the rushing waters in a stream that polish the rocks that lie under the surface.

He gives us flowing rivers of living water. "On the last and greatest day of the feast, Jesus stood up and exclaimed, "Let anyone who thirsts come to me and drink. Whoever believes in me, as scripture says:

'Rivers of living water will flow from within him.'

He said this in reference to the Spirit that those who came to believe in him were to receive." (Jn 7:37-39)

But a more fundamental property of water for the human being is its ability to sustain life. We can do without air for only a few minutes. Then the next thing we need is water (or its substitute). Then would come food and other nourishment. Jesus spoke often of himself as living water which he wishes to give to us, with the promise that we would then never thirst. But he said this in reference to the Spirit, which makes water a reference to the life-giving and sustaining power of the Spirit. Just as we need water to live, so too do we need the Holy Spirit for spiritual life. We use water to cleanse and nourish us: these are images which draw us into the life of the Holy Spirit. (cf. CCC 694)

When the Roman soldiers pierced the side of the expired Jesus on Calvary, both water and blood flowed out. We understand these to be symbols of the mercy of the Sacred Heart of Jesus. It could also be a sign again that the mission of Jesus (to offer his life's blood for our redemption) was accompanied by the mission of the Spirit (to provide life sustaining water).

To provide water for us to carry on our life is surely a work of one who loves us very much. Do you have a holy water font in your home? When you bless yourself with it, you might want to recall that water is a powerful image of the Holy Spirit.

OIL is used in anointing. Hebrew kings in the Old Testament were anointed with oil as a sign of their being so designated by the Spirit, as with David in 1Samuel 16:13: "Then Samuel, with the horn of oil in his hand, anointed him in the midst of his brothers; and from the day on, the spirit of the Lord rushed on David." God also used oil to consecrate the holy tent and its appurtenances as he did with Moses in Exodus 3: 22-32. The Hebrew word "Messiah" and our word "Christ" mean the one anointed by the Spirit. Beginning with Mary's conceiving by the Holy Spirit and all through his life, "the humanity the Son assumed was entirely anointed by the Holy

Spirit." (CCC, 695) In our sacraments of Baptism, Confirmation, Sacrament of the Sick, Holy Orders and Matrimony, oil is used to anoint the recipients as a sign of being fortified by the Holy Spirit.

FIRE in every day parlance is associated with energy; we speak of being "on fire" with enthusiasm for one thing or another. The transmission of energy in the world of religion always connotes an action of the Holy Spirit. John the Baptist was the first to mention that Christian baptism is done with the Holy Spirit and fire. (cf. Lk 1:17, 3:16) Fire consumes and transforms as the Spirit does in transforming life for those who are baptized. As he was nearing the end of his life on earth Jesus complained that not enough people were consumed with the fire of the Spirit: they have insufficient energy; they are not burning with desire to tell the Good News. (cf. Lk 12:49) We also speak of burning with love, so that we ask the Holy Spirit to enkindle in us the fire of his love.

The fire in all these references is only symbolic, though plain enough in their meaning. But there is that other reference to the fire of the Holy Spirit as real flames in the description of his descent upon the apostles and the Blessed Virgin at Pentecost. (cf. Acts 2:3-4) Here there is no doubt that the fire is a physical viewing of the Spirit filling them with himself and immediately empowering them to do things beyond their natural capabilities. There was also the column of fire which protected the Hebrews in their odyssey in the desert, giving light for them to move in the night time. (cf. Ex 13"21)

Why is it important to be on fire? In the book of Revelation, John (writing for Jesus) wrote to the people of Laodocia: "I know your works; I know that you are neither cold nor hot. ... So because you are lukewarm, neither hot nor cold, I will spit you out of my mouth". (Rev 3:15-16)

Ever wonder why one pastor is remembered with more affection than another? Most people are not impressed with erudite sermons, organizational strategies or fund raising success. They just want love from their shepherd.

Fire is also the source of energy. In everyday parlance we speak of someone being on fire with zeal to pursue some objective. We pray that the Spirit's fire will move us to achieve the end for which he created us. Jesus said "I have come to set the earth on fire, and how I wish it were already blazing!" (Lk 12:49)

Fire from earliest times was the source of heat and light. We pray that the Spirit will unfreeze our hardened hearts and warm them up with love and compassion. We pray that he cure our blindness to the needs of others, and that he cast light on all dangers we face in our pilgrimage on earth, and illuminate the way of safety for us.

Being on fire also described righteous anger as it did for Saul in 1 Sam 11:6: "As he listened to this report, the spirit of God rushed upon him, and he became very angry."

Fire is also used to purge, to purify. We pray that the Spirit will cleanse our souls of the stain of sin, as gold is tried by fire.

The DOVE is the symbol most often used iconographically to represent an action of the Holy Spirit. When Noah wished to determine whether the waters covering the earth had subsided, he sent a raven out from the ark. Nothing happened. Next Noah sent a dove which came back to signify the waters had not yet receded. But when he sent the dove second time, the bird returned with a leaf from an olive tree to let Noah know the waters were subsiding. A third time the dove was released and did not return, indicating the Lord had gotten over his displeasure with humans. (cf. Gen 8:10-12) It is not too far fetched to think that the dove was a messenger from the Spirit, since the flood waters are symbolic of baptism, a work of the Holy Spirit.

The most obvious source for the custom of seeing the Spirit in the dove occurred after the baptism of Jesus when the Holy Spirit took the form of a dove to descend upon Our Lord. (cf. Mt

3:16) The dove is considered a gentle, trusting and friendly bird. In some climates, the morning doves will awake you with their loving "coo's". It is also a sign of peace and friendship like the olive branch brought back to Noah. In some churches, the Holy Eucharist is reserved in a metal receptacle shaped like a dove suspended above the altar.

A <u>CLOUD</u> was the constant symbol of the act of the Holy Spirit guiding the Hebrews in their journey through the desert. "The Lord preceded them, in the daytime by means of a column of cloud to show them the way, and at night by means of a column of fire to give them light. Thus they could travel both day and night." (Ex 13:21) Whenever the Israelites camped, the ark was placed in a separate room in a sacred tent, called the Tabernacle. When the Israelites, led by Joshua toward the Promised Land, arrived at the banks of the Jordan river, the ark, over which was a column of cloud, was carried in the lead preceding the people and was the signal for their advance. (cf. Joshua 3:6)

When Jesus was transfigured before Peter, James and John "While he was still speaking, a cloud came and cast a shadow over them, and they became frightened when they entered the cloud. Then from the cloud came a voice that said, 'This is my chosen Son, listen to him.' " (Lk 9:34-35) Here we had the Trinity: Jesus glorified, the Father's voice, and the Spirit in the protecting cloud. That same cloud was to receive the glorified body of Jesus when he rose above the disciples in Acts 1:9.

Conclusion

From all this we must conclude that one of the things that keeps the Holy Spirit busy is firing us up with the fire of his love to energize us to become holy as he commanded us to be, and to keep away from anything that is not of heavenly origin. His love is a force of unity, helping us abide in God and join in Christian love with one another. As our advocate, he is our best friend, walking by our side, giving us comfort and consolation

A BRIEF CONVERSATION WITH THE HOLY SPIRIT

Come, O Holy Spirit, and dwell in my heart.

Come, O Holy Spirit, enkindle the fire of your love in my heart. Melt my frozen heart. Bend my stubborn will. Turn my unruly passions into dirt and ashes. Cleanse my soul of sin.

O Holy Spirit, let me not be lukewarm, but on fire to love you and serve my neighbor. Let me be Spirit-filled! You are by definition the love of Father for the Son and the Son for the Father. Yet you do not keep that love in the Trinity. You bestow love on your entire creation and expect us to bask in it and rest secure in its strength. It has taken me a lifetime to appreciate it, but I finally do: that much as I love you, you have loved me first. The power of your love almost forces me (but you gave me free will) to love you in return. And the superabundance of your love impels me to also love my neighbor. How easy it is, then, to keep the two commandments you gave us through the words of Jesus: love God and love your neighbor.

"Oh God who did instruct he hearts of the faithful by the light of the Holy Spirit, grant us in the same Spirit to be true wise and ever to rejoice in his consolation." (From the perpetual novena to Our Lady of the Immaculate Conception) Give me wisdom — not the ephemeral "smarts" of the mean-spirited, but the eternal knowledge and understanding of your creation and what you want of me. May I also give praise and laud to you for the repose you give me when you calm my worries as I surrender to you and put everything into your hands.

"By your friends you shall know them". I want to treat you as my best friend, indicating what kind of person I am. Peer pressure is something we all have to contend with. Peers are usually the closest friends a person has. If mine are wholesome they will likely influence me to be wholesome too. If they are wicked or unholy, they will have a negative influence on me. With you as my closest friend, O Holy Spirit, I can only wind up holy.

Help me to promote Christian friendship among all I meet so that we can help each other in any kind of necessity.

O Holy Spirit, arouse the missionary and evangelical spirit in the Church so that all may be drawn to the love of Jesus as savior of all mankind.

When I think of you as our comforter, I get a much better idea of the part you play in my life. I think this has been the most significant new understanding I have gained from this, my research into what your work is in my life. I see you now as much more than someone making me a soldier for Christ, much more than someone who inspires and aids me in my life's work. I have seen my beautiful wife as my closest friend, companion, comforter and source of encouragement for these many years. Now I realize that you have been there beside us both, acting in the same way , though hidden and silent. Thank you!

In view of your ceaseless gift of self as love, I need to see the limitations of all that perishes, the folly of the consumerist mindset. Help me, Holy Spirit, to avoid the quest for novelty that so often leaves us wanting and unsatisfied. I am looking for an eternal gift, the spring that will never run dry. Give me the water Jesus spoke of so that I may thirst no more.

You have promised to dwell within me in love. Surround me, I pray, with your loving presence and guard my heart against all that is not holy. Just as in our family we dare not go to bed at night if there are hurt feelings which need to be remedied, I will not close my eyes in sleep until I find a place for you, a dwelling for your strong arm, to paraphrase psalm 132.

I'm convinced, Holy Spirit, that our day is too busy, too frenetic. I need to slow down a bit and try "to be" before I try "to do", as Pope St John Paul II put it. I have learned, Holy Spirit, that I must put aside time each day for private conversation with you. I know the Latin roots of the word conversation, indicate its original meaning was more like "the action of being together among other persons", so less about talking and more about sacred togetherness. Remind me, please, to stop the action with others and just be with you from time to time. As the song says "And he walks with me, and he talks with me, and he tells me I am his alone".

With St. Augustine, I pray: ATTRACT MY HEART, O HOLY SPIRIT, THAT I MAY LOVE ONLY WHAT IS HOLY.

THE HOLY SPIRIT AS HELPER

Strengthen me, O Holy Spirit,
That I may defend all that is holy.

Here Saint Augustine wishes to be given the strength or power, to be given the gifts needed to fulfill his duties. For this he relies on the Holy Spirit, for Jesus told his apostles: "But, I tell you the truth, it is better for you that I go. For if I do not go, the Advocate will not come to you. But if I go, I will send him to you." (Jn16:7) The Bishop of Hippo sees himself as beneficiary of the transformation spoken of by St. Paul to the Corinthians: "'All of us, gazing with unveiled face on the glory of the Lord, are being transformed into the same image from glory to glory, as from the Lord who is the Spirit." (2 Cor 3:18) In terms of the role of the Hoy Spirit, we believe that:

He empowers
He consecrates priests, prophets and kings
He gives charisms
He gives baptism of the Spirit
He helps discernment of one's life work

He empowers

Jesus said clearly at the time of his ascension: "But you will receive power when the holy Spirit comes upon you..." (Acts 1:8)
To empower someone is to give him/her the ability to perform. It begins with the power that sustains, energizes, and keeps us on a holy path. It becomes more specific with regard to

the power or ability to carry out individual tasks. In everyday life some people are given the power to govern when they are elected to office. Others are given the power to exercise a more modest role of oversight through what we call delegation. Still others are given the power to perform specific tasks through appointment, through training or by virtue of finding themselves in a situation calling for action on their part. In all of these occasions, the point is that the individual otherwise would not have the strength, facility or know-how to complete the task without help.

What Augustine seeks is help that permits him to stand up for what is holy. He had his hands full fighting against the heresies of his time. He found the battle to be enervating. He needed his strength constantly in to be renewed. He needed to be sanctified (made holy) himself, and the power to protect that holiness in others.

The Holy Spirit gives us the gift of grace. The word gift suggests being the recipient of something from without. Grace is a sharing in the life of God, and therefore something that we cannot have on our own. It must be gifted to us. That gift is the love of God, the virtue of charity, which, as St. Paul tells us, is supreme to the gift of prophecy, to the gift of miracles, to the science of angels. (cf. 1Cor.13) But he does not stop there. He wants the life of grace to grow within us. Fr. Reginald Garrigou-Lagrange, a noted Dominican theologian of the pre-Vatican II era, compares the initial seed of grace to the mustard seed in Jesus' payable. Grace, he says, "is an embryonic form of everlasting life, the very seed of glory." (From *Knowing, the Love of God: Lessons from a Spiritual Master* by Raymond Smith, O.P.,) The Spirit then cultivates that seed until it becomes large enough so that others can come and rest in our branches.

Scripture is rife with instances of people being thus empowered with a specific ability to carry out a particular task/action. In John 20:22, at the time of his ascension, Jesus gave the apostles the power/authority to forgive sins. Earlier at the last supper, he gave them the power to confect the Eucharist when he said "This is my body, which will be given for you; do this in memory of me." (Lk 22:19) He also had promised: "'You will receive power when the holy Spirit comes upon you, and you will be my witnesses in Jerusalem, throughout Judea and Samaria, and to the ends of the earth." (Acts 1:8)

In this instance, it is clear that the Holy Spirit will be the source of their strength. And help of that sort they will indeed need, for we know how skittish they had become during the Lord's passion, and how timid they were by nature. How could they carry out the mission to preach and baptize all over the world in the face of opposition and danger awaiting them, were it not by being empowered by the Spirit?

We begin to see, then, that another part of the role of the Holy Spirit is that he is the source of whatever empowerment would be necessary to carry out a task desired by God. We can learn more about this attribute of the Holy Spirit from the Old Testament. There we will find numerous examples of empowerment by the Spirit.

Specific tasks calling for special empowerment included the ability for Bezleel to work on the tabernacle as a craftsman. "'I have filled him with a divine spirit of skill and understanding and knowledge in every craft" (Ex 31:3; and repeated word for word in Ex 35:31). The same was true for David to design the temple as an architect: "Then David gave to his son Solomon the pattern of the portico and of the building itself, ... He had successfully committed to writing the exact specifications of the pattern, because the hand of the LORD was upon him." (1 Chron 28:11,19)

He consecrates Priests, Prophets and Kings

The Old Testament empowerment by the Spirit, gifting individuals for service to God's people, was mainly limited to prophets, priests and kings. The Spirit anointed prophets to speak God's word, priests to intercede for the people, and kings to lead the Jewish people against enemies of God. The Lord used all these people to advance his plan of redemption, pointing ultimately to Christ, whom the Spirit also anointed to be Prophet, Priest and King to secure our eternal salvation.

Judges ruled the people of Israel before they had kings. Their accounts in the books of Hebrew history describe them leading the people in battles and in administering justice. The need for wisdom and strength in defeating military enemies called for a specific empowerment by the Spirit. In the case of four of them (Othniel, Gideon, Jephthah and Samson) the empowerment was to carry out the specific task of achieving military victory for Israel. For example, in order for Samson to overcome the Philistines, it was necessary for the Spirit to empower him with extra physical strength to win victory. (cf. Judges 13:25, 14:6, 14:19 and 15:14)

Empowerment was also an important step in making sure various civil rulers of Israel were able to fulfill their leadership role. Even non-Jews could recognize this empowerment, as was the case with Joseph during the years of Jewish captivity in Egypt: "Could we find another like him," Pharaoh asked his officials, "a man so endowed with the spirit of God?" (Gen 41:38) Then we had Moses who was chosen by God to lead some two million Israelites out of Egypt toward the promised land. What was intended to be a relatively short trip turned out to be a forty year odyssey because of the unfaithfulness of the people. This made Moses' job so much more difficult. There is no precise mentioning in scripture of his being empowered by the Spirit, but we know he had it because of the sharing of his power with the seventy elders who joined him in "ruling" the people: "I will come down and speak with you there. I will also take some of the spirit that is on you and will bestow it on them, that they may share the burden of the people with you." (Num 11:17)

Moses was told by God to appoint as his successor "Joshua, the son of Nun, a man of spirit, and lay your hand upon him." (Num 27:18) The kind of strength Joshua needed was not only akin to that of Moses; he also was to wage war against the Canaanites whose land was to be the new home of the Jewish people. When "Joshua fit the battle of Jericho" as expressed in a homespun spiritual melody, he needed the strength to make "the walls come tumbling down".

When Saul became the first monarch style ruler, he was in need of learning how to be a king overnight. Despite his personal weak morality, he was empowered to carryout the task(s) of ruling. Without having to enumerate the many royal tasks undertaken by Saul — from military combat to day-to-day decrees and judicial rulings — we know he was thus empowered by the Spirit: "...Saul, son of Kish, was chosen ... (I Sam.10-21) and "As he listened to this report, the spirit of God rushed upon him and he became very angry." (1 Sam. 11:6)

David was recognized as the successor to Saul, only when "Samuel, with the horn of oil in hand, anointed him in the midst of his brothers; and from that day on, the spirit of the Lord rushed upon David." (1 Sam. 16:13) Recognizing the source of his empowerment, David had seen his father lose the spirit, so he prayed that the same would not happen to him

> "Do not drive me from your presence,
> nor take from me your holy spirit." (Ps 51:13)

He knew how important it was for him to remain empowered, so that he would be a wise king. He mentions another kind of empowerment he received; that is, for his writing:

> "Where can I hide from your spirit?
> From your presence, where can I flee?" (Ps 139:7)

So too for many others of the ancients: Samson, Elijah, Elisha and the other prophets, major and minor alike, including Isaiah, Ezekiel, Daniel, Micah and others. In almost all of these cases it might be noted that these men did not initiate the action of the Holy Sprit by asking for empowerment. It was God who chose these people to be empowered so that his will be done.

So charismatic leadership — a style indicating influence by the spirit — was evident in the leaders of God's people from Moses and the Elders, through the judges and finally to early monarchs. Those kings were anointed with oil, symbolizing being anointed by the Holy Spirit to be empowered to carry out their vocation in a godly way. It would seem, however, that once the Jewish monarchy was passed on through heredity, and not by any special act of God, it lost the gift of the spirit, which then appears to be in the domain of the prophets. The same was true of priests. Too, the prophets of Israel were inspired by the Spirit and equipped to be messengers of God to his people. They gave us sacred scripture in the same basic way that the evangelists did in the New Testament. After them, according to Isaiah, the gifts and powers bestowed on specific individuals in the era before Christ will now be given to the Messianic King. (cf. Is 11:1-2)

When the Spirit "came down" to an individual in the Old Testament, that was not always confirming a person's being in favor with God; i.e., a holy person. For example, Saul was told "The spirit of the LORD will rush upon you, and you will join them in their prophetic state and will be changed into another man." (1 Sam. 10:6) Samson and some of the judges were also not in favor at first. As a result they had the indwelling of the holy Spirit only to perform a specific task. That is in contrast with the New Testament, where the Spirit comes to believers and is permanent.

"If you love me, you will keep my commandments. And I will ask the Father and he will give you another Advocate to be with you always, the Spirit of truth, which the world cannot accept." (Jn 14:15-17) But we need to remember that he can continue to come down as though rekindling dwindling fires.

Charismatic leadership was gradually extended to more than single rulers or leaders. When Moses complained that the burden of leading all the people became so weighty that it was about to crush him, he asked for relief from God. He was told to gather seventy of the elders of Israel in order to take from the Spirit that was upon Moses and distribute it to the seventy so they could help lead the people of Israel. God then gave this charismatic empowering, this special gift, to seventy other people, not just to Moses. Moses' prayer was "Would that all the people of the LORD were prophets! Would that the LORD might bestow put his spirit on them all!" (Num 11:29) The prophet Joel then said that in the latter days that is exactly what would happen. And when the Spirit came on Pentecost, the apostle Peter said it was this about which Joel was writing so that now the Spirit to empower the church for ministries of all kinds is given to everybody, not just to the leaders. This is what we believe happens in the sacrament of Confirmation.

But this power to give power by the Spirit could be shown in dreadful ways when the Lord was displeased We have mentioned how Saul was deprived of his power to rule. There were other occasions with much more devastating repercussions. Isaiah speaks of the spirit's chastising wrath:

> "See the name of the Lord coming from afar
> in burning wrath, with lowering clouds!
> His lips are filed with fury,
> his tongue is like a consuming fire;
> His breath like a flood in a ravine
> that reaches suddenly to the neck,

Will winnow the nations with a destructive
winnowing…" (Is 30:27-8)

This is how Yaweh shows his anger:

"The Lord shall dry up the tongue of the sea of Egypt,
and wave his hand over the Euphrates in his
fierce anger
And shatter it into seven streams
so that it can be crossed in sandals." (Is 11:15)

We should not be misled into thinking that the Spirit mentioned so often in the Old Testament is different from the Holy Spirit as we speak of him in the New Testament. They are one and the same third Person of God, as is evident from the words of Jesus and the apostles. For example: "David himself, inspired by the holy Spirit, said…" (Mk 12:36); and "My brothers, the scriptures had to be fulfilled which the holy Spirit spoke beforehand through the mouth of David, concerning Judas…" (Acts 1:16) and

"Therefore, as the holy Spirit says:
'Oh, that today you would hear his voice…'
" (Heb 3:7)

Before we leave this examination of empowerment recorded in scared scripture, we must mention Isaiah's prophecy about the Spirit empowering the life and ministry of Jesus. We read: "The Spirit of the LORD shall rest on him" (Is 11:2), inspiring God's Chosen One with wisdom, understanding, counsel, might, knowledge, fear of the Lord, righteousness and faithfulness (cf. Is 61:1,2). Jesus himself told the people that he was the fulfillment of this prophecy (cf. Lk 4:18,19). We, of course, continue to receive the same gifts of the Holy Spirit, itemized as knowledge, understanding, wisdom, counsel, fortitude, piety and fear of the Lord. (CCC, 1831)

A logical question that might come to mind at this time concerns the timing of empowerment vis-a-vis details as to what the plan of action was to be for the one so fortified. In most cases, God through the Spirit called an individual and then spoke of a job to be done, a message to be sent or some action to be taken. However, when Jesus was about to ascend into heaven after his resurrection, he commissioned the apostles giving them the details about the baptism of all people in the name of the Father and the Son and the Holy Spirit. But he then told them not to begin doing this until he sent the Spirit to empower them. So the plan came first and the empowerment later in this case.

So it seems to be with most callings today. Individuals spend years studying how to minister, how to rule, how to teach, and then if found worthy, they are commissioned formally or publicly to do so. It seems one has to desire and work toward being empowered for specific work and not be selected from on high out of the blue, so to speak. There may be a lesson here for those in Christian communities of our day who are asked to prepare themselves for answering a call to work in promoting the message of the Gospel (i.e. to teach religious education) or performing some ancillary role in liturgical celebrations (e.g., to serve as a lector, a server, or a special minister).

He gives Charisms

We have seen that among the results of being infused with the Holy Spirit are abilities beyond the natural limits for humans, such as speaking in tongues and prophesying. To differentiate these special favors of the Spirit from what are called his seven gifts, the word charism is often used when speaking of supernatural powers, as in CCC, 1508 "The Holy Spirit gives to some a special charism of healing...(1 Cor 12:9, 28, 30)". Such outward manifestations of the

Spirit working with believers comes with temptations to be either arrogant in their use or jealous in recognizing them in others.

This was something that bothered St Paul and caused him to write to the people of Corinth. These early adherents to the new Way were blessed with many outward signs of the indwelling of the Spirit. Paul warns them not to be envious of a gift given to someone else. Paul mentions three powers to speak (tongues, interpretation and prophesying; three powers to do (healing, miracles and faith) and three powers to know (knowledge, wisdom, and discerning of spirits). (1 Cor 12: 8-11) All come from the same Holy Spirit; all are intended to be used for the benefit of the community. All are needed for the building up of the Church.

After listing these, St Paul goes on in chapter 13 of 1Corinthians to say such charisms are to be accepted with thanks by the person receiving them and by the entire community. They will help build up the Church provided they are used in conformity with authentic promptings of the Holy Spirit, that is "in keeping with charity, the true measure of all charisms". (cf. 1 Cor 13)" (CCC, 800)

Paul had also heard there might be some untrue special powers being claimed to the detriment of the peace of the community, He therefore cautioned that all charisms were subject to the authentication by the shepherds of the Church. Such a process was intended not to extinguish any valid gift of the Spirit, but to ensure that all the diverse charisms work together for the common good. Today's clergy must be gifted with "faculties", or the power to perform their ministry in a given locale, by the local bishop to protect the people.

He gives Baptism of the Spirit

In a rare occurrence, all four evangelists, and Luke again in the book of Acts, use almost the exact same words to speak of the baptism of John compared with the baptism of Jesus and of

Pentecost. It is clear that the baptism of the Spirit and fire does not refer to a baptism of repentance like that of John the Baptist. All of the evangelists make this point.

> "I am baptizing you with water, for repentance, but the one who is coming after me is mightier than I. I am not worthy to carry his sandals. He will baptize you with the holy Spirit and fire." (Mt 3:11)
>
> "I have baptized you with water; he will baptize you with the holy Spirit. (Mk 1:8)
>
> "John answered them all, saying, 'I am baptizing you with water, but one mightier than I is coming. I am not worthy to loosen the thongs of his sandals. He will baptize you with the holy Spirit and fire." (Lk 3:16)
>
> "John testified further, saying 'I saw the spirit come down like a dove from the sky and remain upon him. I did not know him, but the one who sent me to baptize with water told me, 'On whomever you see the Spirit come down and remain, he is the one who will baptize with the holy Spirit' ". (Jn 1:32-3)
>
> "...for John baptized with water, but in a few days you will be baptized with the holy Spirit." (Acts 1:5)
>
> "... and I remembered the word of the Lord, how he had said, 'John baptized with water but you will be baptized with the holy Spirit' " (Acts 11:16)

Baptism with water cleans the soul of original and actual sin; persons baptized are now saved; they have recognized and accepted Jesus as their personal Savior. Then a further indwelling of the Spirit takes place with what is often called baptism by the Spirit and fire. Catholics and many other Christian groups refer to this as the sacrament of Confirmation, But it could be called a second baptism, because the word "baptism" in Greek simply means a drenching or overflowing or being inundated or totally suffused, which is what takes place by the laying of the hands by the bishop or other cleric.

Such is what took place when St Paul found some believers in Ephesus. In answer to questioning, they said they had never heard of the Holy Spirit but had been baptized with the baptism of John. Paul then baptized them with the baptism of Jesus. And when Paul laid his hands on these twelve men "the holy Spirit came upon them, and they spoke in tongues and prophesied." (Acts 19:6)

Something similar happened when St Peter spoke to Cornelius, a God-fearing man, and his whole household in Caesarea—only in reverse order. While Peter preached to them, the Spirit came down upon them, and they were heard speaking in tongues and glorifying God. (cf. Acts 10:46) They were Gentiles and this surprised Peter. But seeing what had happened, Peter could not withhold baptism with water from them — but the baptism of the Spirit had happened first.

Philip's ministry to the people of Samaria also showed the difference between baptizing with water and then being baptized by the laying on of hands (cf Acts, chapter 8). The laying of hands brought about such spectacular gifts that a man named Simon, a magician, offered money to St Peter for the power to lay hands. Which caused the irascible Peter to exclaim "May your money perish with you..." (Acts 8:20), as this ritual was not a show but a religious activity: a sacrament, or outward sign of the imparting of grace.

Speaking in tongues seems to have been the surest sign of being infused by the Holy Spirit. Which is what prompted St

Paul to say to the people of Corinth: "Now I should like all of you to speak in tongues" (1 Cor.14:5), that is, to be baptized by the Holy Spirit. "... "the effect of the sacrament of Confirmation is the full outpouring of the Holy Spirit as once granted to the apostles on the day of Pentecost." (CCC, 1302)

Jesus showed that he too was imbued by the Spirit in general, but also carried out specific ministries by being empowered by the Holy Spirit. As the Word of God, Our Lord was totally wrapt up with the Holy Spirit as part of the Trinity which had no beginning nor end. As Jesus, his human nature was baptized by John the Baptist (Lk 3:21-22). Then whenever he began episodes of his ministry, he attested that he is doing so by the power of the Holy Spirit. Thus he said he was preaching by the power of the Holy Spirit (cf. Lk 4:18-21); he cast out devils by the power of the Holy Spirit (Mt 28); and why he cured on the Sabbath. (cf. Mt 12:9-13)

It should also be noted here that before Jesus began any of the major events in his life, he spent considerable time in prayer. Asking for empowerment? Maybe. But more aptly to be sure that he and the Father remained in each other. A model for us all, of course. Pope St. John Paul 11 was clear in reminding us of this, especially because of the times we live in. Writing in his encyclical on the coming new millennium, he wrote: "It is important, however that what we propose, with the help of God, should be profoundly rooted in contemplation and prayer. Ours is a time of continual movement, which often leads to restlessness, with the risk of 'doing for the sake of doing'. We must resist this temptation by trying 'to be' before trying 'to do'." (Novo Millennio Ineunte #15)

Jesus is God. He is all-knowing; he is all powerful; nothing is impossible for him. Yet when it came time for him to pass on to his disciples his mission of bringing salvation to the world, he always did so by giving them the Holy Spirit. When he appeared to the apostles right after his resurrection: "[Jesus] said to them again, 'Peace be with you. As the Father has sent me, so I send you.' And when he had said this, he breathed on them and said to them, 'Receive the holy Spirit. Whose sins you forgive are forgiven them, and whose sins you retain are retained.' " (Jn 20:21-22)

When Jesus ascended to heaven he told the apostles not to leave Jerusalem but to wait for the promised advocate. He told them they would be baptized by the Spirit who would strengthen them for their task. "But you will receive power when the holy Spirit comes upon you, and you will be my witnesses in Jerusalem, throughout Judea and Samaria, and to the ends of the earth." (Acts 1:8)

He helps discernment of one's life work

We have considered numerous examples of the Holy Spirit empowering individuals, especially in the Old Testament, to perform specific tasks of leadership, prophesying and priestly ministry. But what about the choice of a whole profession or life's work? Discernment of what one's state in life should be is a perilous activity. Choosing the wrong one — one for which you are not qualified or in which you will scandalize others, or otherwise be a failure — would be a terrible waste.

How can we be prevented from making such a mistake?

From earliest times, God himself intervened and directly chose individuals to a calling. In Genesis 12: 1-2, we hear God choosing Abram, one of the sons of Terah, and telling him "Go forth from the land of your kinsfolk and from your father's house to a land that I will show you. I will make of you a great nation, and I will bless you…."

Likewise, when Moses saw a bush on fire but not burning, and decided to investigate, "God called out to him from the bush, 'Moses! Moses!' He answered, 'Here I am'." (Ex 3:4)

In the first book of Samuel, God clearly made the choice for Samuel by calling him not once, not twice, but three times, and telling him what was expected of him. (1 Sam 3:8)

In the case of Israel's kings, it is clear these were appointed, reluctantly, by God to take his place in leading his people. Priests have always been seen as taking the place of God in the assembly, either as according to the line of Melchizedek in the Old Testament, or as other Christs in the New Testament. As for prophets, the Spirit is the mouth of God speaking through the mouths of humans, and he is the hand of God through the hands of scripture authors who command, warn, promise, teach and exhort humankind.

In like manner, Isaiah was assured of what his call was when, in chapter six "I heard the voice of the Lord saying, 'Whom shall I send? Who will go for us?' 'Here I am', I said; 'send me!' And he replied 'Go and say to this people:...' " (Is 6: 8-9)

Later, when God speaks to Israel in Isaiah, chapter 43:1-4, he says

> "I have called you by name: you are mine. ...
> Because you are precious in my eyes
> and glorious, and because I love you..."

Being called by name is not something to fear. It is not just a call to perform some duty like being selected by lot from an induction list at the Draft Board. God calls me by name because he loves me and finds me precious.

I belong to him, when he adopts me at baptism and I am given a name that he can then recognize. How important it is that I be given a name by my parents that will ring a chord with God. Yet how we have lost the technique of giving our children a Christian name. You will notice that Muslims are very careful to name their offspring with a Mohammedan name, but some of us name our children after movie stars, sports heroes, rock stars or other celebs, etc.

What's in a name? Christ told Simon "And so I say to you, you are Peter, and upon this rock I will build my church." (Mt 16:18) And Peter had a new life's work: to be a fisher of men.

In Acts 9:4, Saul was called by being thrown to the ground by a brilliant light and was directly told by Christ, whom he had been persecuting, to change his life's work.

In Acts 13:2, Barnabas and Saul were sent to the right place for their ministry by the choosing of lots guided by the Holy Spirit.

These are some of the more notorious examples of being called to a life acceptable to God. All this has led to the concept of being "called" to what might be considered God's holy work. But all work is holy if done in a manner pleasing to the eyes of God, which is what we all wish to do with our lives as given to us by the Spirit.

Men and women today who choose the priesthood or religious life apply for such a life's work and study what such a life entails. But only when they are officially "called" to their vows can they be assured they are making the right choice. For then they will hear: "It was not you who chose me, but I who chose you..." (Jn 15:16)

Most of us must be guided by the Spirit in a less formal way in choosing our life's work or state of life (married or single), or employment. We begin by acknowledging that we need help. This prompts us to want help, to pray for it, and ultimately to trust or expect that we will receive that help. This is a process that takes time as many find out unfortunately by hastily responding to first offers or unfounded self assessments. If it is a matter of gainful employment that we seek, there are numerous agencies, books or other resources to assist in the search. This is not the place to go into detail about that. Suffice it to say that there is much need for the divine Helper in such a mundane decision.

The bottom line is to trust in the Holy Spirit to want to protect the life he gave to us, as long as we put our future in his loving hands.

Conclusion

In both the New and Old Testaments, the source of empowerment is clearly the Holy Spirit. It must be concluded that this is one of the attributes that should be included in any list we seek to make as particular to the third Person of the Blessed Trinity. A special function of the Holy Spirit is to provide the help necessary to fulfill one's mission by empowering those who are called. And as Christians we are all called to spread the Good News in one way or another. The divine Helper is ready, willing and able to gift us with the knowledge, skills and fortitude to fulfill our life's work. This in turn prepares us to do battle for all that is holy. There is no other way to be holy, which is the challenge for us all, and to champion all those who are holy.

A BRIEF CONVERSATION WITH THE HOLY SPIRIT

Come, O Holy Spirit, and empower me to fulfill my duties.

Holy Spirit, helper of the weak, I look to you for help in this process of personal sanctification first: to die to my old self and be all that God created me to be; to be free from the slavery of sin and the entanglement of things of this world. Make me more like my Messiah, who, after all, received his very life from you.

Spirit of God, how magnificent is your ability to empower us poor humans. You have taken shepherds and made them kings; you have taken peasants and made them prophetic messengers like your angels; you have taken simple followers of the law and made them priestly intermediaries with your people. I am reminded of the words of Gabriel to the Blessed Virgin: "Nothing is impossible for God". Jesus used these same words when speaking to Peter who has just kind of complained that he and the other apostles had given up everything to follow the Lord.

How often have I, almost instinctively, called upon you for the strength to resist temptation, for the enlightenment to know your will, for the courage to undertake difficult tasks, for the empowerment to carry out duties, both simple and difficult. Jesus told his disciples "Do not worry about what to say in times of persecution, for it will be given you (by the Spirit) what to say." And how often has that been true in my case. When facing examinations, when called upon to speak in public, when asked to solve a problem, to reconcile the estranged, or select from many options — you have always been there for me. And sometimes I forgot to say Thank you!

Discerning a true calling is no easy matter. Yet you have told us to pray for light, and for courage, and for determination to succeed once a choice has been made. And so it has worked out for me time after time. You are still the empowering Spirit, showing the way forward, shading light on unknown circumstances, giving the strength to endure through troubling times. As the years pass and I find my major responsibilities changing, please empower me with the new talents required at this stage of my life.

Now that I see how much I really owe you for successful completion of so many tasks, please help me to recognize the sinful pride with which I have taken credit for so much of your work through me. Forgive my conceit, my arrogance, and my egotism in not giving you credit for your empowerment. I see athletes on the field raise their eyes and give victory signs to thank you when they are successful. They are not ashamed to give you credit for their prowess. May I learn to do the same in recognizing you as the "power behind the throne" of any success I may have.

Just as it is true that I need your life-giving power to sustain the life you gave me, so too I need your help in being able to carry out the mission you have given me, Too often have I forgotten that the work, the duties, the responsibilities I have constitute a calling or mission from you and that you want to work by my side as a true helper.

Help me to understand that any empowering that you do for me is not to deepen my own spiritual life; Its focus is on others. This is help you are giving me to perform a task. It is always concerned with protecting or deepening the relationship between you and any people I might serve in your name. I trust you will find me faithful if I use what you give me fruitfully and deign to give me some reward when I come before you in judgment; but that is something extra.

With St. Augustine, I pray: STRENGTHEN ME, O HOLY SPIRIT, THAT I MAY DEFEND ALL THAT IS HOLY.

THE HOLY SPIRIT AS PROTECTOR

Protect me then, O Holy Spirit,
That I may always be holy.

This last verse seeks the guidance, the protection, the way of life that is lived by a holy person. Here Saint Augustine pleads for a permanent relationship with the Spirit. He does not want to lose the state of grace. As Doctor of Grace, he treasures his call to holiness and sees this as a lasting need. This in turn called for protection from veering off course. In terms of the work of the Holy Spirit, we believe that:

> He takes up his dwelling within us
> He protects from illness and suffering
> He guides along the way
> He provides strength
> He rescues us
> He protects the true faith

He takes up his dwelling within us

The focus of this plea of Augustine is one of permanence. The lasting relationship of the individual with the Holy Spirit is often referred to as his indwelling. It should be noted that this is one area where the role of the Spirit in the Old Testament varies from his "work" in the New Testament. In 1 Cor 3:16-17, St. Paul mentions the permanent indwelling of the Holy Spirit in believers. Belief in Christ causes the Holy Spirit to live within us. In Ephesians 1:13,14 Paul calls this permanent indwelling the "guarantee of our inheritance". This is very different from the language we find in the Old Testament where the indwelling was selective and temporary. The Spirit "came upon" people like Joshua (Numbers 27:18), David (1 Sam.16:12,13), and Saul (1 Sam 10:10). The indwelling was a sign God's favor upon that individual. If the person's behavior caused God's favor to leave him, the Spirit would depart, as with Saul in 1 Sam.16:14.

It is said that the Church is the temple of the Holy Spirit, meaning he dwells within it The individual believer is likewise the temple of the Holy Spirit. "Do you not know that your body is a temple of the holy Spirit within you, whom you have from God...?" (1 Cor 6:19) It's a bit mind-boggling to think that God lives in us. But Jesus promised "the Spirit of truth … remains with you, and will be in you." (Jn 14:17) This calls for constant fellowship with the Holy Spirit, and being aware of his presence with us at all times. He is a person, one of the three in the Trinity. He will talk to you. Allow yourself to be led by the Spirit.(cf. Gal 5:18) This calls for submission to his directions, to his will. We must permit him to direct our lives. "If we live in the Spirit, let us also follow the Spirit." (Gal 5:25)

The word "dwell" is used to describe someone's permanent residence in a place. You do not dwell in a vacation home. You do not visit someone and dwell there. In like manner your "dwelling" is your permanent home. Your overnight stay in a hotel is not your dwelling. If your are on an expedition somewhere, you do not take up your dwelling there.

Augustine is seeking a protection or guidance that will keep him holy for always. You make sure your dwelling is adequately safeguarded. You use locks and fences and alarms. You pay for police and fire protection. You seek permanent safety You can then feel secure. With this assurance, you can devote yourself to the life or work at hand, knowing you are protected from intrusion. This is what Augustine pleas for here: the permanent residence of the Spirit in his heart so that he can carry out his mission to become holy.

He protects from illness and suffering

One obvious need for protection of the life given by the Holy Spirit concerns protecting it from sickness. We read in James 5:14: "Is anyone among you sick? He should summon the presbyters of the church, and they should pray over him and anoint [him] with oil in the name of the Lord." Oil here is a type of the Holy Spirit; hence healing is a "work" of the third person off the Blessed Trinity, carrying on the work of the second person who has now ascended into heaven.

There are those who think that since we are taught to accept the will of God even if it means suffering, we should just embrace the suffering assigned to us. But this is not the will of God. Nowhere does the gospel record that Jesus instructed people simply to bear the suffering assigned to them. In no case does he indicate that a person is asking for too much and should be content with a partial healing or no healing at all. He invariably treats illness as an evil to be overcome rather than a good to be embraced. Illness, after all, is a result of original sin.

Jesus does not always respond immediately to the demands of the needy crowds. On a few occasions he withdraws to be alone with his Father in prayer and then to move on to his next destination. It is also reasonable to infer that Jesus did not cure every every sick person within reach. At the pool of Bethsaida, for example, there lay a multitude of invalids, blind, lame, paralyzed, but the gospel mentions his speaking to, and curing, only one lame man. Scripture does not say that the Lord will always heal in response to our prayer if only we have enough faith, though Jesus often did ask for an admission of faith before effecting a cure.

There are also instances in which Jesus initially seems to refuse a request, but then in response to persistent faith he does perform a miracle. However the gospels record no instance in which a person asks for healing and is categorically refused. This evidence from Scripture ought to challenge our accustomed ideas about the Lord's will to heal. Have we too often accepted the idea that sickness should simply be embraced? Do we too easily assume that if a person is ill, God wants things to stay that way for good? Could our resignation to illness or infirmity even sometimes be a cloak for unbelief? Jesus instructs his followers not only to visit the sick but also to heal them. Not every one who bathes in the waters of Lourdes is cured. However, it is reasonable to conclude that the Lord desires to heal far more often than we think. Hence we invoke the Holy Spirit to exercise his "function" of protecting us from illness and suffering.

In the administration of the Sacrament of the Sick, the Priest (or deacon) prays that the Holy Spirit will lay his hands on the infirm and restore them to good health. The Holy Spirit is seen as the loving actor representing the Trinity in curing illness and protecting from physical harm. His guidance is sought for all the health-care professionals who might minister to the sick. His comfort is asked for so that all the loved ones of the sick be protected from worry and be a source of consolation for the ill.

Our prayers to the Holy Spirit for the sick and suffering should be constant and not limited just to those we happen to know. "Let them (all Christians) pray also that the strength and consolation of the Holy Spirit may descend copiously upon all those many Christians of whatever Church who endure suffering and deprivations for their unwavering loyalty to the name of Christ." (Vatican Council II, *Decree on Eastern Catholic Churches*, #30)

I feel the need to mention in particular those who have mental diseases. As people tend to live longer, there are more and more cases of dementia, alzheimers and parkinsons sickness.

In advanced cases, people suffering from these diseases lose the use of their reason. Their mind wanders; they cannot focus; they do not know where they are or what they suffer from. We are saddened by the loss of their ability to carry on the kind of conversation they formerly did. It seems to be such waste of mental capabilities. They even seem unable to ask for divine intervention. We must pray for the work of the Holy Spirit, who controls thoughts, in their stead.

He guides along the way

When Moses led God's people out of Egypt (i.e., the Exodus) he was only a figurehead leader. We know from Exodus 14:19 that it was "the angel of God, who had been leading Israel's camp". The angel and the column of cloud left their place in front and went to the rear of the fleeing Israelites to protect them from the pursuing Egyptians. But is was Isaiah who identified the angel of God as the holy Spirit:

> "It was not a messenger or an angel,
> but he himself who saved them" (Is 63:9).

And

> "Whose glorious arm
> was the guide at Moses' right
> … the spirit of the Lord guiding them" (Is 63:12-14).

Jeremiah instructed the people: "Let the LORD, your God, show us what way we should take and what we should do." (Jer 42:3)

From the beginning of the new Way, it was the Holy Spirit who guided the new Christians in carrying out their duties. "They traveled through the Phrygian and Galatian territory because they had been prevented by the holy Spirit from preaching the message in the province of Asia." (Acts 16:6) And "When they came to Mysia, they tried to go on into Bithynia, but the Spirit of Jesus did not allow them..." (Acts 16:7)

What this guidance involves has been very clearly stated by the Vatican Council in the *Dogmatic Constitution of the Church*, #4, including the scriptural source for each, as follows: "The Sprit dwells in the Church and in the hearts of the faithful as in a temple (cf. 1 Cor 3:16; 6:19). In them he prays and bears witness to the fact that they are adopted sons (cf. Gal 4:6; Rom 8:15-16 and 26). The Spirit guides the Church into the fulness of truth (cf. Jn 16:13) and gives her a unity of fellowship and service. He furnishes and directs her with various gifts, both hierarchical and charismatic, and adorns her with the fruits of His grace (cf. Eph 4:11-12; 1 Cor 12:4); Gal 3:22). By the power of the gospel He makes the Church grow, perpetually renews her, and leads her to perfect union with her Spouse.. The Spirit and the Bride both say to the Lord Jesus, 'Come!'. (cf. Apoc 22:17)"

One of the most significant aspects of the guidance we receive from the Holy Spirit concerns his guidance in recognizing good versus evil. As Jesus prepared the apostles for his coming passion and death, he wanted to leave them with confidence in their ability to live the life he had trained them in. He told them about the Advocate who would take his place, and emphasized this discerning power of the Spirit using somewhat strange terminology. "I will send him to you. And when he comes he will convict the world in regard to sin and righteousness and condemnation." (Jn 16: 7-8)

These words needed clarification, so Jesus explained: "... sin, because they do not believe in me; righteousness, because I am going to the Father and you will no longer see me; condemnation because the ruler of this world has been condemned." (Jn 16:9-11) In the canticle "Veni, Creator Spiritus" the Spirit is given the title "Light of Hearts", which is to say he gives light to our consciences. The Spirit convinces or sheds light concerning sin. He gives us guidance to see right from wrong.

He convicts or passes judgment on us, helping us to realize our own evil and gives the ability to choose good.

Because we are body and soul, we are constantly fighting a battle to see which of these will carry a given day or even win the final battle. We find in St. Paul a clear picture of the two sides: "I say, then: live by the Spirit and you will certainly not gratify the desire of the flesh. For the flesh has desires against the Spirit, and the Spirit against the flesh; these are opposed to each other, so that you may not do what you want." (Gal 5:16-17) We just cannot avoid feeling a certain tension, a struggle between Spirit and flesh.

Did you ever pick up a flashlight and suddenly realize you have not used it in some time, leaving you with dead batteries? Our spiritual batteries can get run down too. One aspect of the guidance of the Holy Spirit is that he does not just fill us with himself once and then leave us to our own devices. No. "Be filled with the Spirit" (Eph 5:18). This verse actually means keep being filled. It is not a one time experience, but a daily refill, a recharge of our spiritual battery because of our innate weakness.

> "For he knows how we are formed,
> remembers that we are dust." (Ps 103:14)

Remember how both Jahweh and Jesus posited the dichotomy between life and death, with the plea: choose life! There are those who would have you believe there is no Spirit, no human soul made after the image and likeness of God. For them there is no choosing to be done. Man is doomed because of the mortality of his flesh to end up dead with no possibility of an after life. Blindness of judgment is one of the effects of sin.

How despondent a view of life because of no appreciation of the work of the Holy Spirit.

St. Paul prays that God let his Spirit help believers to mature beyond such a belief. "For this reason I kneel before the Father that he may grant you in accord with the riches of his glory to be strengthened with power through his Spirit in the inner self."

(Eph 3: 14-15) He paints a very different picture of what lies ahead for those who believe in the goodness of the Spirit.

> " 'What eye has not seen, and ear has not heard,
> and what has not entered the human heart,
> what God has prepared for those who love him,'
> this God has revealed to us through the Spirit."
> (1 Cor 2:9-10)

We call this having an upright conscience. The Vatican II document *Gaudium et Spes*, or *The Church in the Modern World*, Par 27, spells out in clear language the difference between good and evil so there can be no misinterpretation: "whatever is opposed to life itself, such as any type of murder, genocide, abortion, euthanasia, or willful self-destruction, whatever violates the integrity of the human person, such as mutilation, torment inflicted on body or mind, attempts to coerce the will itself; whatever limits human dignity, such as subhuman living conditions, arbitrary imprisonment, deportation, slavery, prostitution, the selling of women and children; as well as disgraceful working conditions, where men are treated as mere tools for profit, rather than as free and responsible persons; all these things and others of their like are infamies indeed." Having called by name the many different sins that are so frequent in our time, the Council concludes that these poison human society and do more harm to those who practice them than to those who suffer from the injury. Call this a modern explanation of the fifth commandment "Thou shalt not kill".

He provides strength

Listen to St. Paul indicate clearly where strength comes from. As a minister of God's grace, he tells the Ephesians "I kneel before the Father, from whom every family in heaven and on earth is named, that he may grant you in accord with the riches of his glory to be strengthened with power through his Spirit in the inner self." (Eph 3:14-16)

We have seen that a quick summary of what happened to the apostles at Pentecost is to say they were strengthened and made courageous to go forward with their mission. The repeated baptism by the Spirit in succeeding months and years of the new Church, as reported repeatedly in the Acts of the Apostles, provided the strength that was needed to carry on the mission of Jesus now that he had returned to the Father. That was the work of the Holy Sprit at that time and is the same work he continues to perform in guiding the Church of Jesus Christ.

"Confirmation begins an increase and deepening of baptismal grace... it increases the gifts of the Holy Spirit within us..." And "it gives us a special strength of the Holy Spirit to spread the faith by word and action as true witnesses of Christ, to confess the name of Christ boldly, and never to be ashamed of the Cross. (cf. Council of Florence [1349]; LG 11; 12)" (CCC, 1303)

Most Catholics receive the sacrament of Confirmation in their early teens. Probably a good time for it, since the teen years introduce young minds and hearts to a barrage of new experiences of life based on the development of puberty and of their intellect.

Through this sacrament, we receive a filling of the Holy Spirit which makes us soldiers of Christ. It gives us the strength to courageously live the Gospel in our homes, neighborhoods, parish communities and civil societies. We thus are able to fulfill our purpose by proclaiming the Good news and inviting all people to encounter the love and mercy of Jesus Christ.

The coming of the Holy Spirit generates faith in the believer. In Hebrews, chapter eleven, St. Paul explains how many of the ancients were prompted by faith to believe what God had promised with regard to their redemption would come to pass. So Abel and Enoch and Abraham and Isaac and Jacob and Esau and Moses and Gideon and Samson and David and Samuel are all mentioned as having been able to carry out their mission by the faith they received from God. Paul is making the point that even though all these heroes of the Old Testament had kept the faith and often endured mockery, scourging, imprisonment, stoning, beheading and death by other means, the strength to endure all this discipline from God — they did not receive what they had been promised, that is, a Savior. He encourages us to pray for it is only to those who have accepted Jesus as our personal Savior who receive strength for our "drooping hands and weak knees" (Heb 12:12). Granting such strength is the "work" of the Holy Spirit.

The sad thing then is that the special strength of the sacrament peters out. This will come as no surprise. For our entire life we find it necessary to renew our strength, both of body and of mind. You can hardly turn on your television set without seeing a commercial extolling the power of this, that or some other machine to keep your body in good shape. It's either that or another one pleading with us to drink orange juice — or nowadays beet extract — in order to retain our strength. We all accept the need for a healthy diet and good exercise to provide the strength our bodies need. Well, guess what?! The same is true for our spiritual life. How often have the saints told us that there is no standing still in our growth in holiness: we either keep going up or we start sliding back. So where do we go to find the elixir for holiness? St Augustine offers his prayer as a good place to start.

He rescues us

No mater how valiant we are in trying to follow the guidance of the Holy Spirit there are times when the onslaught of Satan and his never ending battle to win over those who love God, becomes too much for our feeble defenses and we fall. Coming to our senses, we realize the Holy Spirit is there to rescue us, to tend to the broken bones and elevated blood pressure of our spiritual life. He might be thought of as our friendly emergency room doctor, anxious to remedy our trauma.

As we hope physical emergencies are rare, so we pray that spiritual disasters do not happen; but our fallen nature is always in danger, so we call on the Holy Spirit as the love of Christ:

> "You are my shelter; from distress you keep me;
> with safety you ring me round.
>
> … But the Lord's eyes are upon the reverent;
> upon those who hope for his gracious help;
> Delivering them from death,
> keeping them alive in times of famine. (Ps 32:7 and 33:18-19)

He protects the true faith

Jesus rose from the dead on the first day of the week. That same evening he appeared to the apostles to let them know he had risen. He knew they were distraught about his passion and death, so much so that they were cowering in a locked room for fear of what might happen to them as followers of Jesus. He wished to comfort them and relieve their anxiety as to where his body was. But he did not spend any time discussing any of that. He seemed to have something very important on his mind For, after shocking them by his sudden appearance and wishing them peace, he immediately got down to business. He was about to commission them. "As the Father has sent me, so I send you." (Jn 20:21)

Later when he was about to ascend into heaven, he would give the specific command to go and baptize others to the end of the world, but he had first to empower them to have confidence that what they would be preaching would be the true faith as he had established it. So on the very day of his resurrection, Jesus appeared to ten of the apostles, wished them to be at peace, then "breathed on them and said to them, 'Receive the holy Spirit. Whose sins you forgive are forgiven them, and whose sins you retain are retained.'" (Jn 20:22-23) Simply put, Jesus put them in the hands of the Spirit to know the difference between right and wrong, of true repentance and lack of true faith. Or, put in another way, the Spirit would protect the true faith of his church through the judgment of his apostles and those who came after them.

It is noteworthy to point out that this is one of only two times that God breathed on man, the other being in Genesis 2:7 when the Spirit created the first human life. This action of Jesus emphasizes how important this protection was for his church.

Another time Jesus appeared to a small group of his disciples, seven in number, along the shore and invited them for breakfast. After they had finished, he said to Peter "Simon, son of John, do you love me more than these?" (Jn 21:15) Peter answered in the affirmative. Three times in the self-same words, Jesus asked the question: do you love me? Then, hearing Peter's affirmation of love three times, the Lord commanded him each time "Feed my sheep." (Jn 21:17) Why go through this three times? Jesus was affirming the choice of his successor on earth. He was affirming Peter to be the shepherd of his new church. That was why he carefully called Peter by his given name three times. There must be no question as to who was to be the leader.

Affirming, because earlier, before his passion and death, Jesus declared who would be the stable protector of the Church, when Jesus said to Peter "... you are Peter and upon this rock I will build my church, and the gates of the netherworld shall not prevail against it. I will give you the keys to the kingdom of heaven. Whatever you bind on earth shall be bound in heaven; and whatever you loose on earth shall be loosed in heaven." (Mt 16: 18-19)

This had already been set up as the succession to follow Jesus. But Peter and the others became weak, even to the denial of knowing the Lord, which is why Jesus had to give them the Holy Spirit when things calmed down a bit and they were ready to begin their evangelizing mission.

It then becomes interesting to follow how the Holy Spirit monitors and leads Peter and the others in the work assigned to them. For example, there is the episode concerning Cornelius, a centurion of the court. This man had lived a good life, devout and god-fearing. He had a vision of an angel of the Lord telling him to go and summon Peter. At the same time Peter was praying on the roof top of the house where he was staying, having his own vision of food being sent from heaven for him to eat. When the message from Cornelius came, Peter was considering what to do, and "...the Spirit said [to him]: '.. get up, go downstairs and accompany them without hesitation, because I have sent them.' (Acts 10:19-20)

This work of the Spirit is to protect the church of Jesus Christ from straying from the true faith as Jesus had established it. Each year we celebrate the feast of the Chair of St Peter as a reminder of this. We are not celebrating a piece of furniture; we are celebrating a very important theological concept. The chair signifies the continuing love of Jesus for his church by the establishment of the papacy to govern his church lovingly until his second coming. Jesus did not abandon his Church when the ascended to heaven; he established a living tradition of teaching, governing and sanctifying: all under the protection of the Holy Spirit. When the pope and the body of bishops exercise their teaching authority, the faithful must assent to their judgments "as pronounced with the assistance of the Holy Spirit." (Vatican II, *Dogmatic Constitution on the Church*, #25) This is the Church we are to love and follow. Augustine saw this clearly when he said: "A man possesses the Holy Spirit to the measure of his love for Christ's Church." (*Sermons on John*, 22, 8)

By giving the keys to the kingdom to Peter and by giving the apostles the power to forgive sins through the protection of the Holy Spirit, Jesus' sacrament of reconciliation would be protected in his church. He did the same for the sacrament of his precious Body and Blood. "At the center of the church is the Eucharist where Christ is present and active in humanity and in the whole world by means of the Holy Spirit." (Pope Saint John Paul II, general audience, Sept. 1989) The Eucharistic liturgy is saturated with the presence of the Holy Spirit. The close collaboration of Jesus with the Holy Spirit continues in this sacrament. "At the heart of the Eucharistic celebration are the bread and wine that, by the words of Christ and the invocation of the Holy Spirit, become Christ's Body and Blood." (CCC, 1333)

Thus in the Eucharistic Prayer number two the priest says. "You are indeed Holy, O Lord, the fount of all holiness. Make holy, therefore, these gifts, we pray, by sending down your Spirit upon them like the dewfall, so that they may become for us the Body and Blood of our Lord Jesus Christ."

Jesus promised "But when he comes, the Spirit of truth, he will guide you to all truth." (Jn 16:13) The Second Vatican Council, reflecting on these words in the *Dogmatic Constitution on Divine Revelation*, tells us that this applies to us all, for the Holy Spirit leads unto all truth those who believe and makes the word of Christ dwell abundantly in them. And in another document: "For it is the function of the Church, led by the Holy Spirit who renews and purifies her ceaselessly, to make God the Father and His

Incarnate Son present and in a sense visible." (Vatican Council II, *Pastoral Constitution on the Church in the Modern World*, #21)

Having received the Holy Spirit on Pentecost, the apostles then fulfilled their mission by their preaching and by their holy lives based on the promptings they received from the Holy Spirit. The Spirit was the principle of their coming together and remaining together in the teaching of the apostles and in fellowship, in the breaking of the bread, and in prayers. (cf. Acts 2:42) It was he who then built up the Church of Christ and inspired some of them to put in writing the Good News. (cf. Jn 20:31; 2 Tim 3:16; 2 Pet 1:19-21 and 3:15-16) After them, the bishops of the Church received the Holy Spirit and became authentic teachers and shepherds of the faithful. At the same time, "the lay person should learn to advance the mission of Christ and the Church by basing his life on belief in the divine mystery of creation and redemption, and by being sensitive to the movement of the Holy Spirit who gives life to the People of God and who would impel all men to love God the Father as well as the world and mankind in Him." (Vatican Council II, *Decree on the Apostolate of the Laity*, #29)

Our present holy father, Pope Francis, challenged us as follows in his general audience catechesis on May 13, 2013: "Let's ask ourselves: are we open to the Holy Spirit, do I pray to him to enlighten me, to make me more sensitive to the things of God? And this is a prayer we need to pray every day: Holy Spirit may my heart be open to the Word of God, may my heart be open to good, may my heart be open to the beauty of God, every day. But I would like to ask a question to all of you: How many of you pray every day to the Holy Spirit? Eh, a few of you I bet, eh! Well, a few, few, a few, but we realize this wish of Jesus, pray every day for the Holy Spirit to open our hearts to Jesus."

We probably cannot say enough about the role of the Holy Spirit in protecting and building up the Church of Christ. When Jesus ascended into heaven, his command to his disciples was to go and baptize <u>all</u> people in the name of the Trinity. He knew his little band of ragamuffins was notoriously lacking in knowledge, in strength, in courage, so he sent the Holy Spirit to provide these traits and everything else they might need to carry out their assignment. It was the Holy Spirit who was to oversee the spread of the kingdom world-wide. So his descent at Pentecost was not for a short visit. He came and stayed! (cf. Jn 14:16)

The Holy Spirit protects the authenticity of our faith by his own direct actions; but he also works through the various elements that make up the structure of the Church. Recognizing this, and aware of the need to give reminders periodically, the Council fathers at Vatican II took pains to comment on the need to hearken to the inspiration of the Holy Spirit in several of their decrees on renewal. They said the Holy Spirit:

- instructs bishops to manifest love in the pastoring of souls (cf. the *Decree on the Bishops' Pastoral Office in the Church, #1);*

- *suggests and fosters fitting adaptati*ons to the ministry of priests i(cf. the *Decree on the Ministry and Life of Priests, #22*);

- recommends family life in religious communities (cf. the *Decree on the Appropriate Renewal of Religious Life, #15*);

- insists on an attitude of service in the formation of seminarians (cf. the *Decree on Priestly Formation, #9*);

- "Led by the Holy Spirit, Mother Church unceasingly exhorts her sons to purify and renew themselves so that the sign of Christ can shine more brightly on the face of the Church." (*Pastoral Constitution on the Church in the Modern World, #43*)

Some of the faithful have still not reconciled themselves to the changes in the liturgy mandated by that same Vatican

Council II. Maybe some of us are just slow learners, but it might help if we simply recall that the attempt to "restore" the liturgy is one sign, along with many others, that evidenced itself to the bishops as a movement of the Holy Spirit in his role of protecting the integrity of the Church of Jesus. (cf. Vatican II, *Constitution on the Sacred Liturgy*, #43)

Conclusion

Protect, guard, guide, strengthen, fortify, rescue, pardon, help, be a refuge, show mercy—the list goes on and on. All these actions are what we think of when we consider this function of the Holy Spirit. And from the permanent need for all of these on the part of the Holy Spirit, we must conclude that protecting is one of the most important of his attributes. He does so by a permanent indwelling, by constant reinvigorating, and by cautious guidance and protection against straying from the tenets and virtues established by Jesus Christ in his Church.

A BRIEF CONVERSATION WITH THE HOLY SPIRIT

Come, O Holy Spirit, and fortify me to complete my spiritual journey.
"The best defense is a good offense." A good strategy against a foe on the field of sports, and against a spiritual foe anxious to derail us on our way to eternal happiness. That might suggest that we should arm ourselves against evil and evil doers by fortifying ourselves with your protection, O Holy Spirit, as you offer yourself as a guard, a shield, a barricade, a fortress. We don't wait until we are flailing in distress—we call on you to lead us through perils of all kinds and furnish us with righteousness in advance of being attacked. The devil hates a holy person, and

will surely come after us, so I pray to you in advance: Guard me then, Holy Spirit, that I may always be holy.

O Holy Spirit, in order to obtain a new mind, I consecrate and give my will to you in exchange for your divine will. I truly want your divine will to generate its divine life in me this day — to think in all my thoughts, to speak in all my words and operate in all my actions for the glory of our heavenly Father and to fulfill the purpose of creation. ... I love you with your own will and thank you profoundly for the knowledge and gift of the divine will. (From the prayer of Servant of God Louisa Picaretta)

May the will of the Father, made known in Jesus, by the power of you, Holy Spirit, reign in me through Mary.

You shield us from harm; teach me to protect goodness in ourselves and others.

You guard us against stumbling and help us from falling; strengthen my reliance on you in every temptation.

You are the shelter fall those who are in need; make me a shelter to all who call upon me for help.

Guide me, O Spirit, in the way of your commands. In your statutes I will delight; let me not forget the words of your scriptures. Give me discernment that all my choices be pleasing to you.

> "I will always hope in you,
> and add to all your praise.
> My mouth shall proclaim your just deeds,
> day after day your acts of deliverance,
> though I cannot number them all." (Ps 71:14-15)

Your ways are faithfulness and love, for which I should give thanks and praise, but I seem most of the time to be forgetful of your being my leading light. Forgive me.

Holy Spirit, dwelling within me as in a temple, how rarely I remember that you are so close to me. How rarely do I take the time to converse with you who are ever anxious to show me what the next step should be as you guide me along the way! Please forgive my inattentiveness.

With St. Augustine, I pray: PROTECT ME, O HOLY SPIRIT, THAT I MAY ALWAYS BE HOLY!

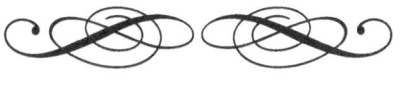

A Final Word...

We have been researching what the prayer of St. Augustine might teach us about what the Holy Spirit does for us. We have drawn mainly from sacred scripture in both the Old and New Testaments where we see him in action. Hopefully the Spirit has become much closer to us as a companion who animates our spiritual life as we answer God's command to "be holy because I am holy". (cf. Lev 11:44 and 1 Pet 1:15)

A vibrant prayer life is an essential element in being holy. The Church quoting Our Blessed Lord, tells us to pray always. One simple way of doing that we are told in the catechism is to have the name of Jesus on our lips always (CCC, 2665-69). As the hymn puts it "Jesus in the morning, Jesus at the noon time, Jesus when the sun goes down". But "Every time we begin to pray to Jesus it is the Holy Spirit who draws us on the way of prayer." (CCC, 2670) It is the Holy Spirit acting within us that makes prayer possible: "He is the artisan of the living tradition of prayer" (CCC, 2672)

But many are afraid to pray or think they have to be a living saint before they can pray, etc. We need to overcome this weakness of mind. "The Spirit too comes to the aid of our weakness; for we do not know how to pray as we ought, but the Spirit itself intercedes with inexpressible groanings." (Rom 8:26) We seem to be in the arms of a catch-22 here: The Holy Spirit will help us to pray; but we are reluctant to pray for the gift of the Spirit. So we must make a habit of saying frequently "Come, Holy Spirit". (CCC, 2671) These are the first words of the sequence at the Mass of Pentecost in the Roman Missal: "Come, Holy Spirit, fill the hearts of your faithful and enkindle in them the fire of your love". One of the first things we should pray for is the gift of the Holy Spirit. "If you then, who are wicked, know how to give good gifts to your children, how much more will the Father in heaven give the gift of the holy Spirit to those who ask him?" (Lk 11:13)

We have also been taught that the Church perseveres in prayer with Mary. We should always remember gratefully that there is a special relationship between Mary and the Holy Spirit. He was responsible for her original sanctification in her Immaculate Conception. He overshadowed Mary, thus conceiving her beloved Son, Jesus. He inspired her wonderful Magnificat when Elizabeth's child leapt in her womb. He inspired the holy man Simeon to prophecy that Mary's heart would be pierced with a sword. He descended upon her along with the apostles at Pentecost and all the times the disciples gathered in prayer to begin founding Jesus' Church. He exercised his power in assuming Mary into heaven body and soul.

"The more the Holy Ghost finds Mary, his dear and inseparable spouse, in any soul, the more active and mighty he becomes in producing Jesus Christ in that soul and that soul in Jesus Christ." (*True Devotion to Mary* by Saint Louis deMontfort, #20)

When you pray your rosary and come to the third glorious mystery, you have an opportunity to reflect on all we have reviewed concerning what the Holy Spirit does for us. Remembering the specific event (Pentecost) that is the focus of this mystery is the beginning of praying this decade. If you close your eyes you might imagine the Holy Spirit as a dove descending to take up his place in your heart. Or imagine the flames that settled on the heads of the Apostles resting also on your head as a reminder to be on fire filling you with joy and love. Recalling how the Spirit comes to you and how thankful we are for his visit and constant presence as your paraclete (i.e., friend, companion, consoler, etc.) will help keep your recitation of the rosary more devout.

Let us say with fervor "I believe in the Holy Spirit" and know what we mean. We are unceasingly professing our faith that we created beings are being aided in becoming holy by an eternal gift, who is the Holy Spirit, third Person of the Blessed Trinity: uncreated, without limit, omnipotent, ours only for the asking: "Come, Holy Spirit..." Amen

www.ingramcontent.com/pod-product-compliance
Lightning Source LLC
LaVergne TN
LVHW040152080526
838202LV00042B/3131